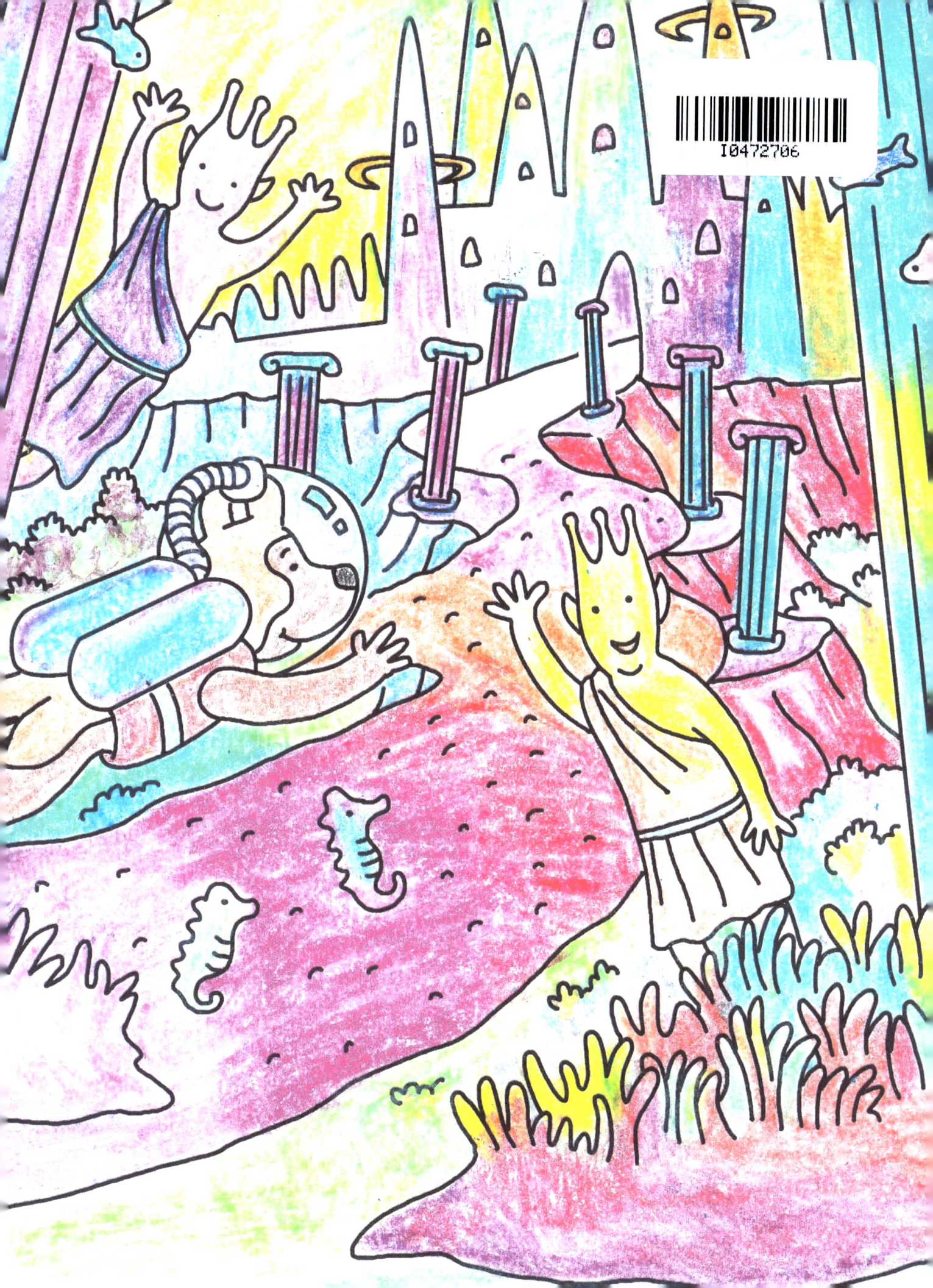

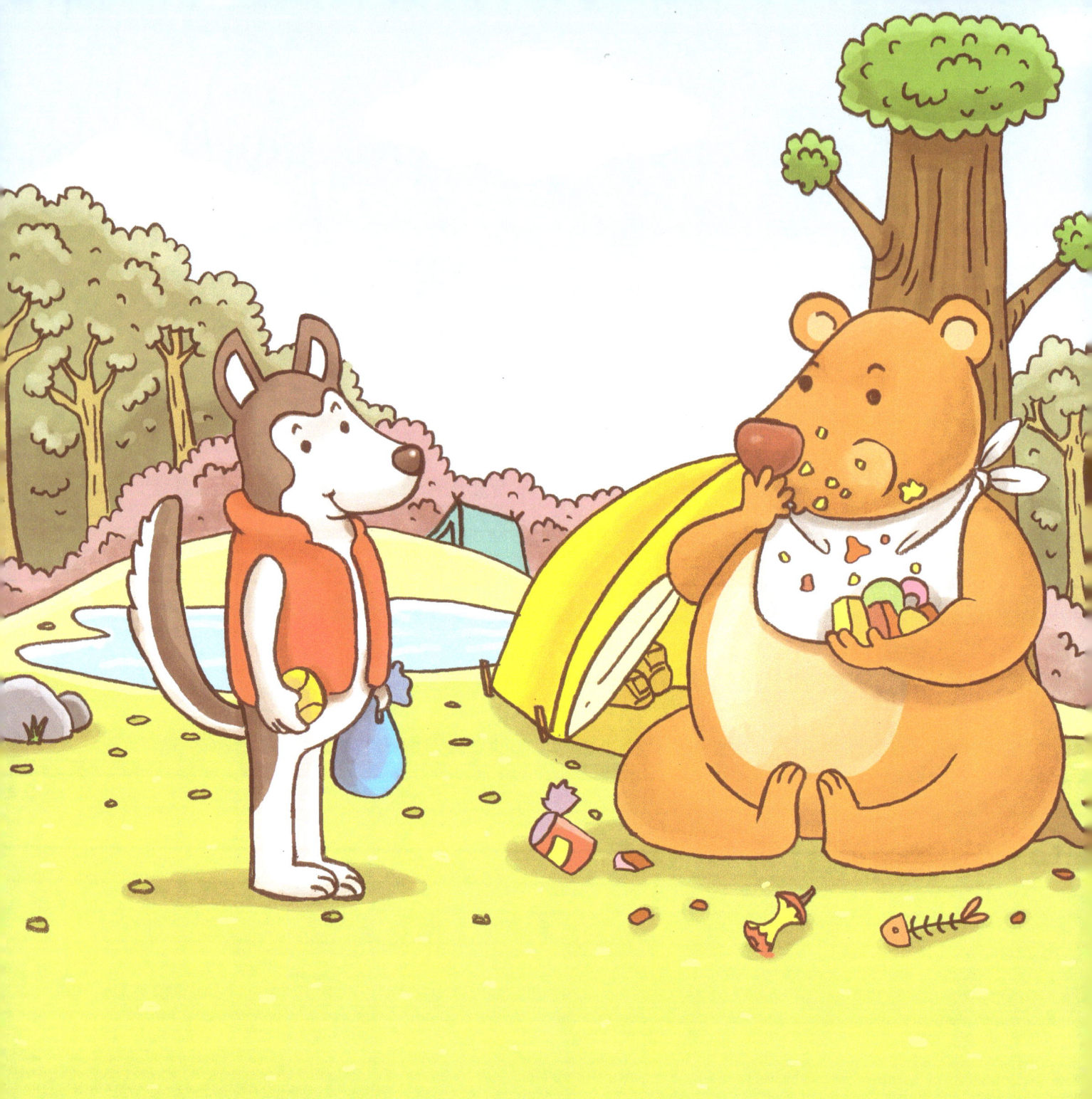

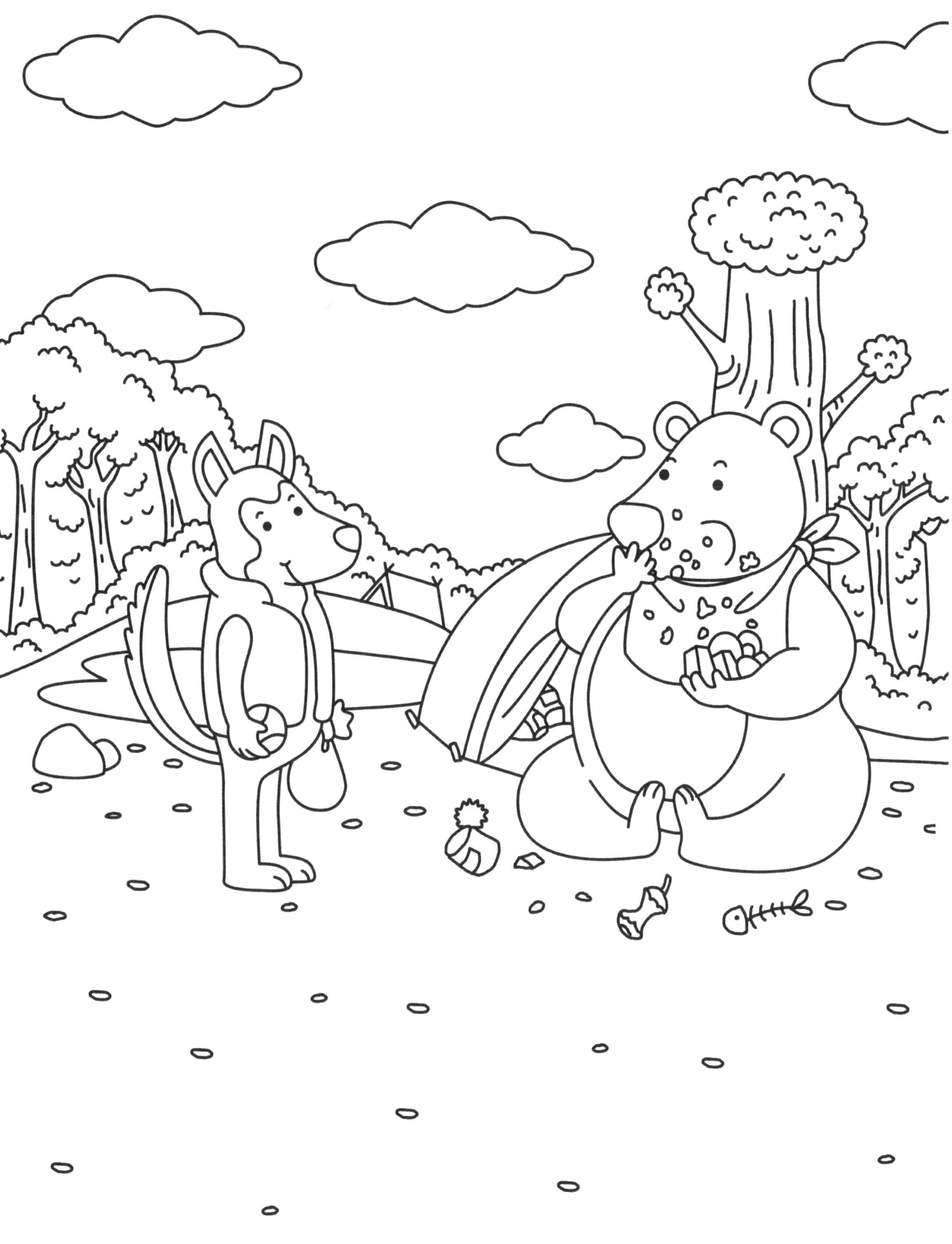

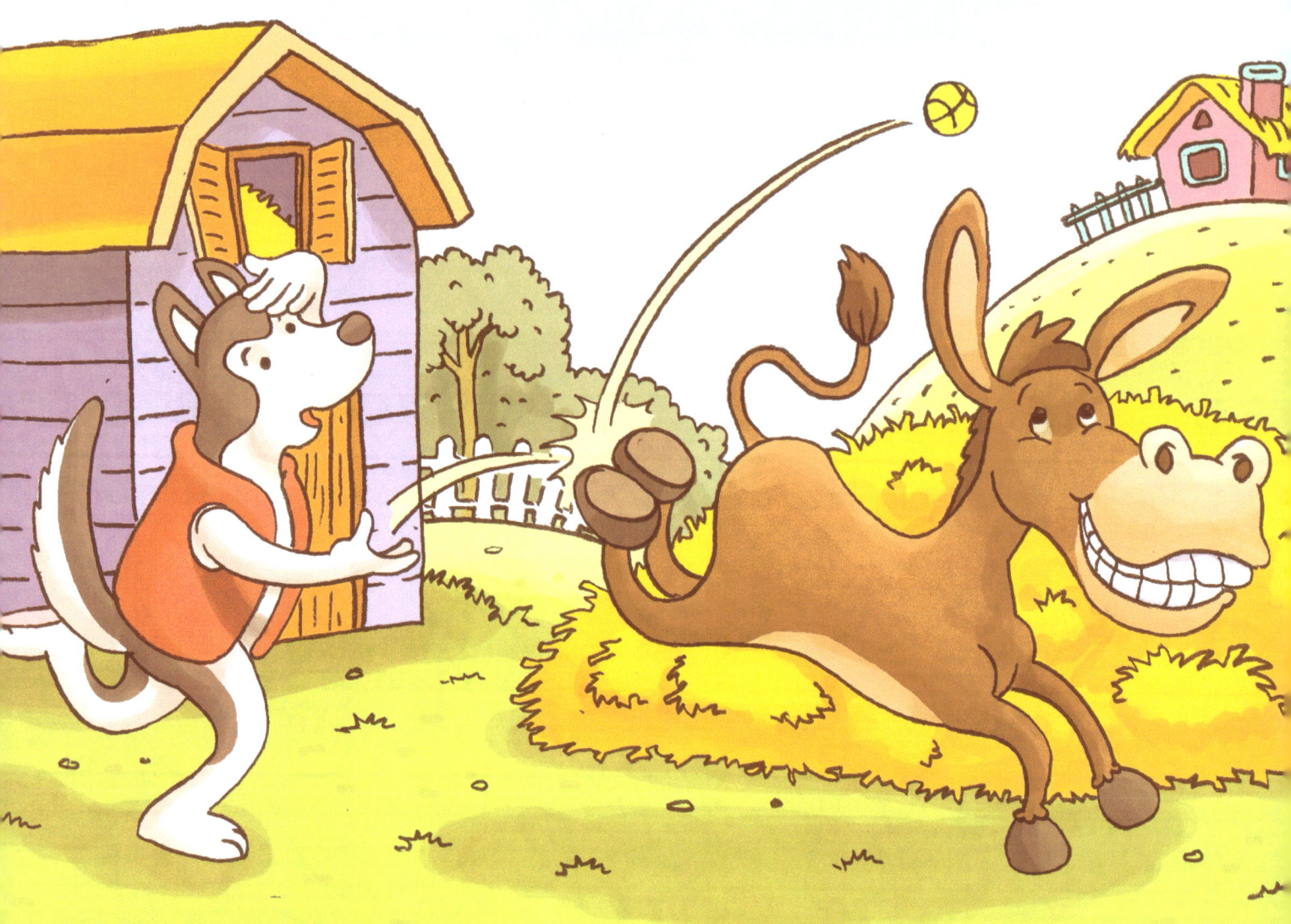

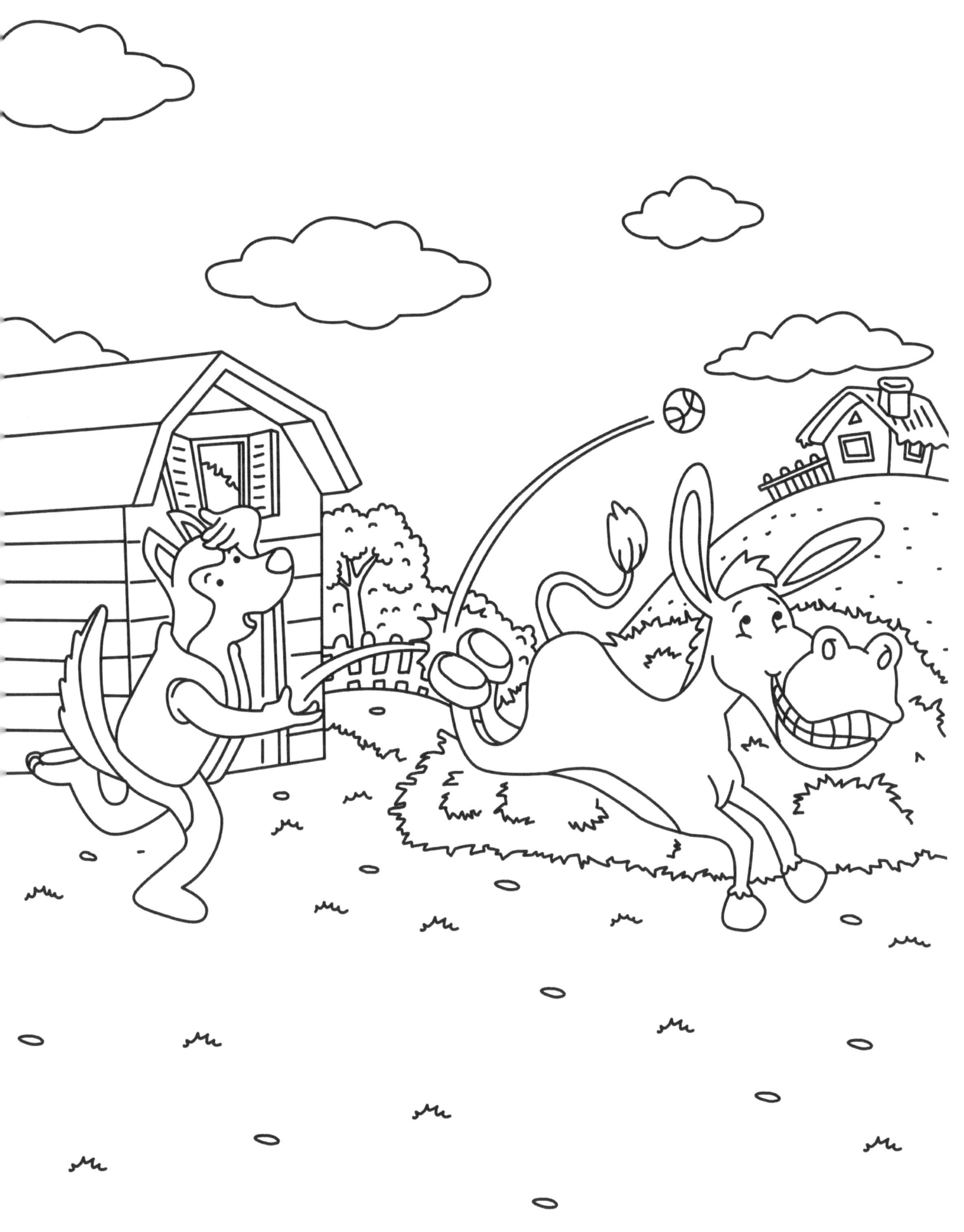

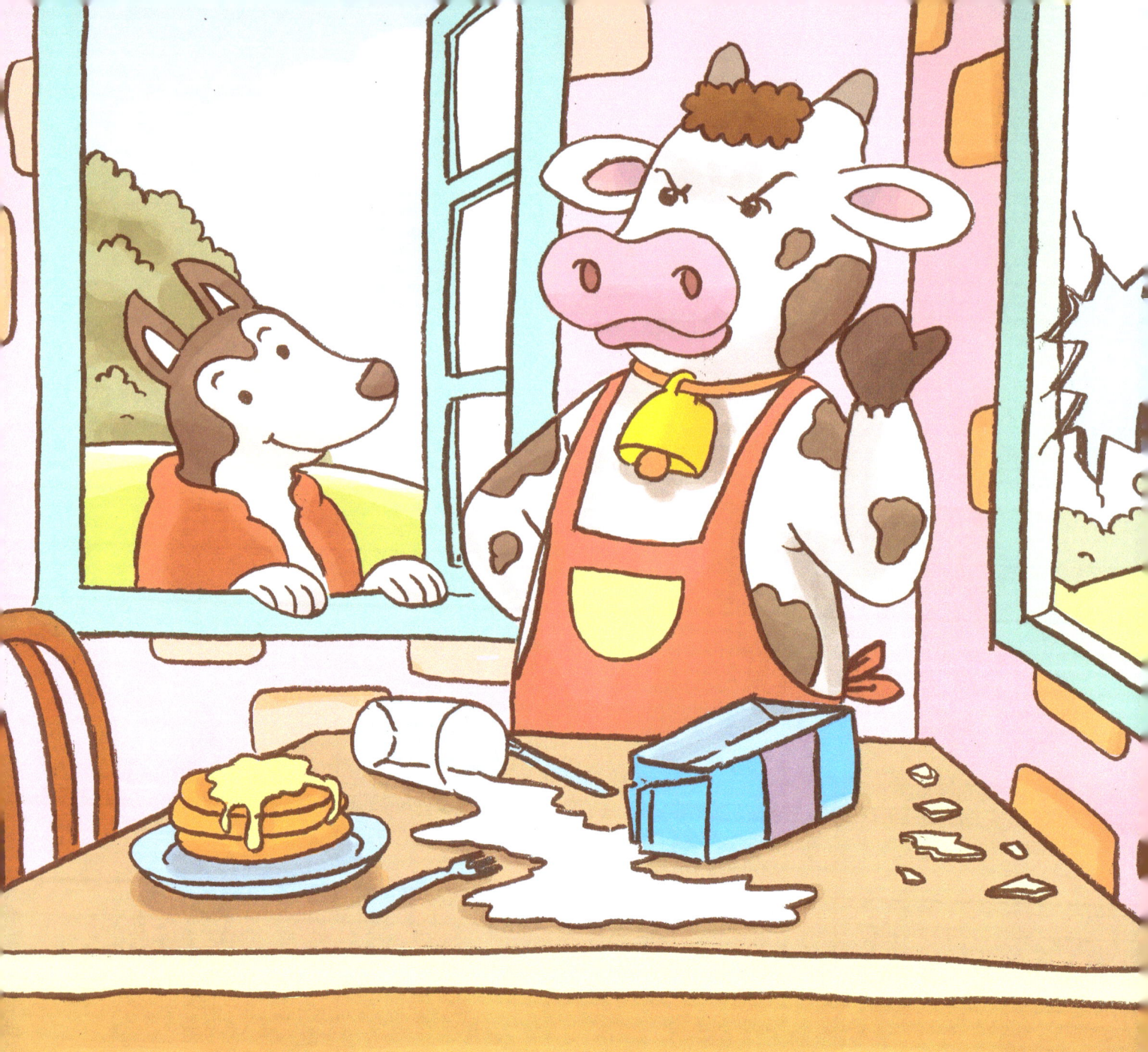

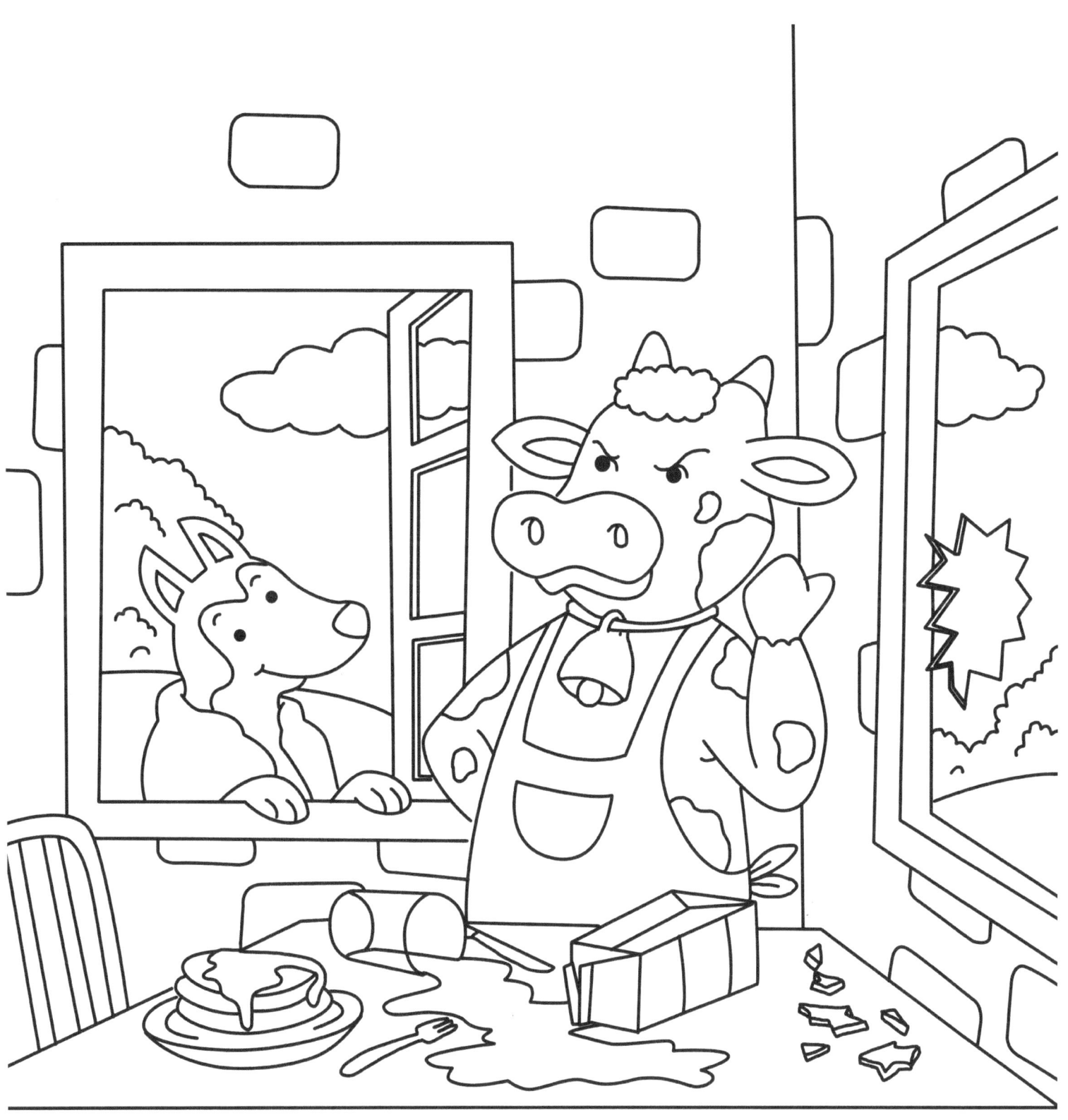

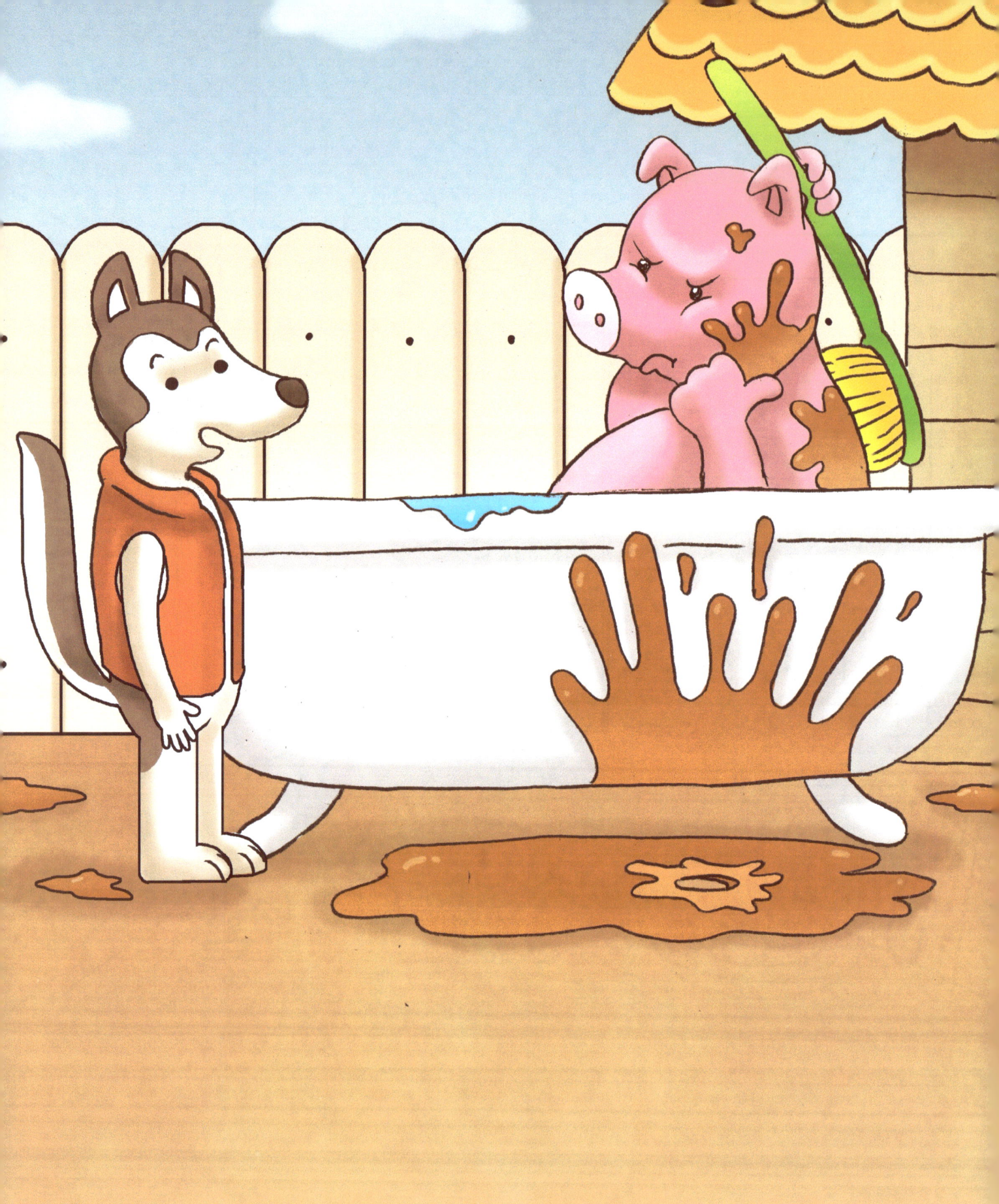

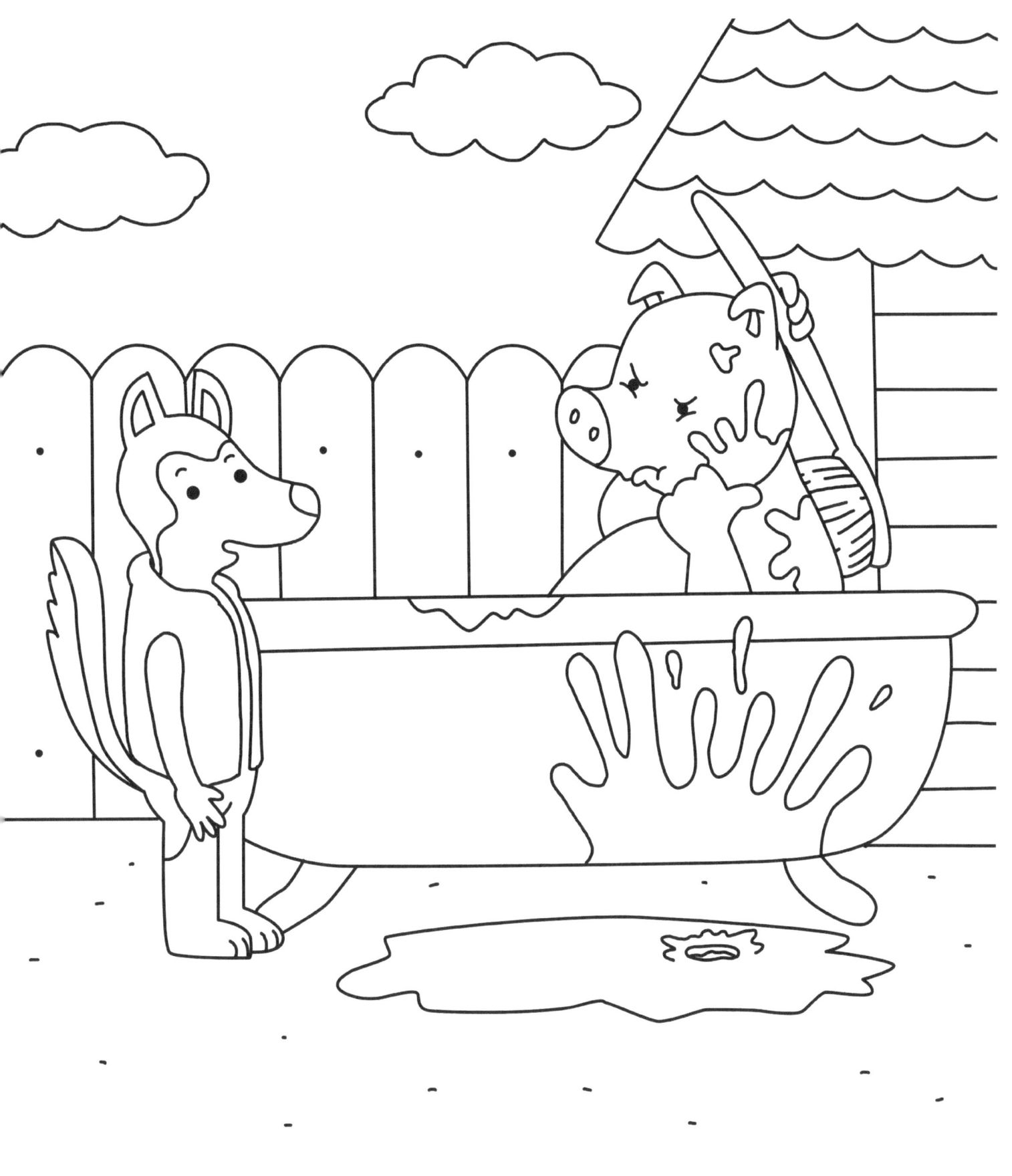

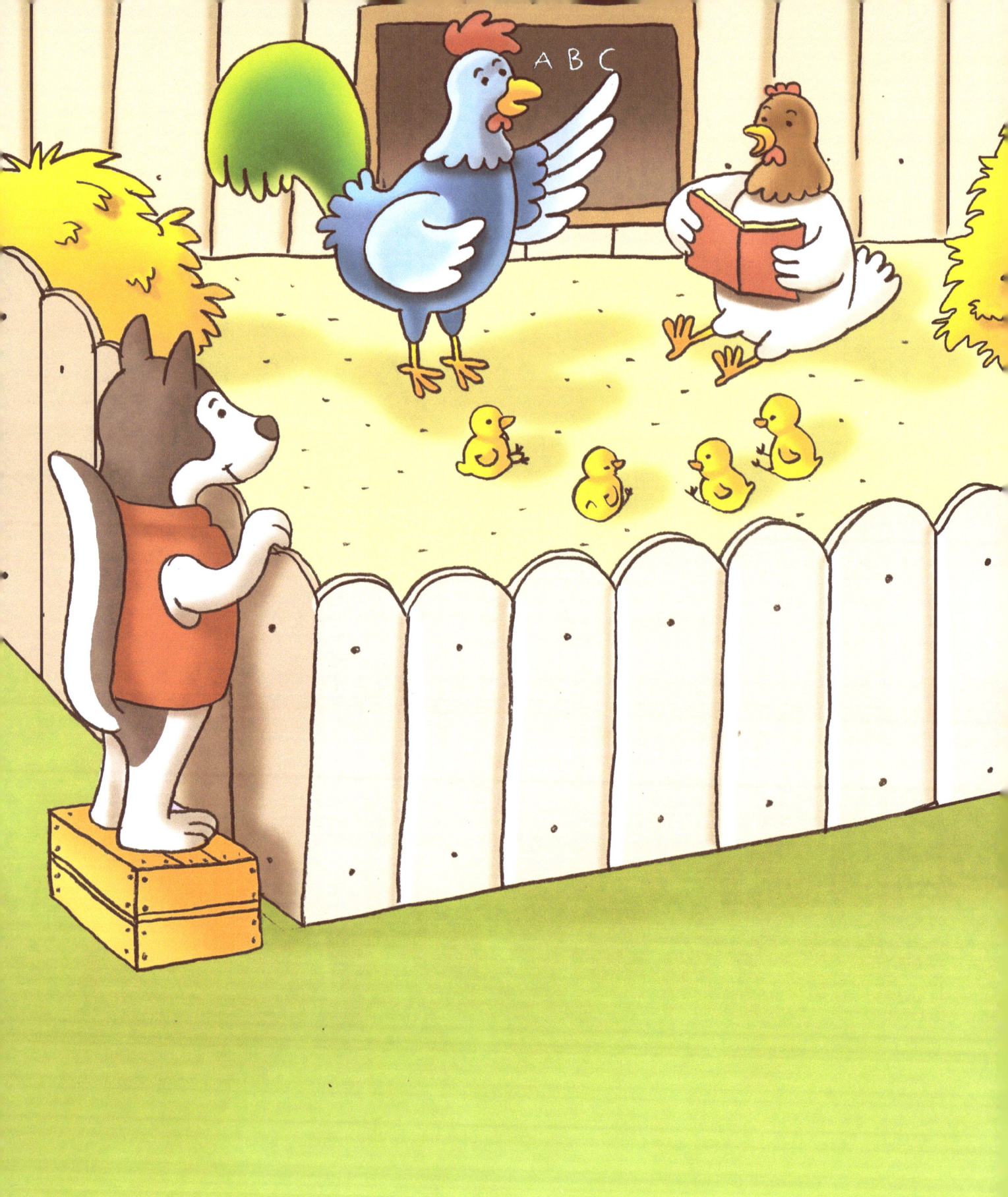

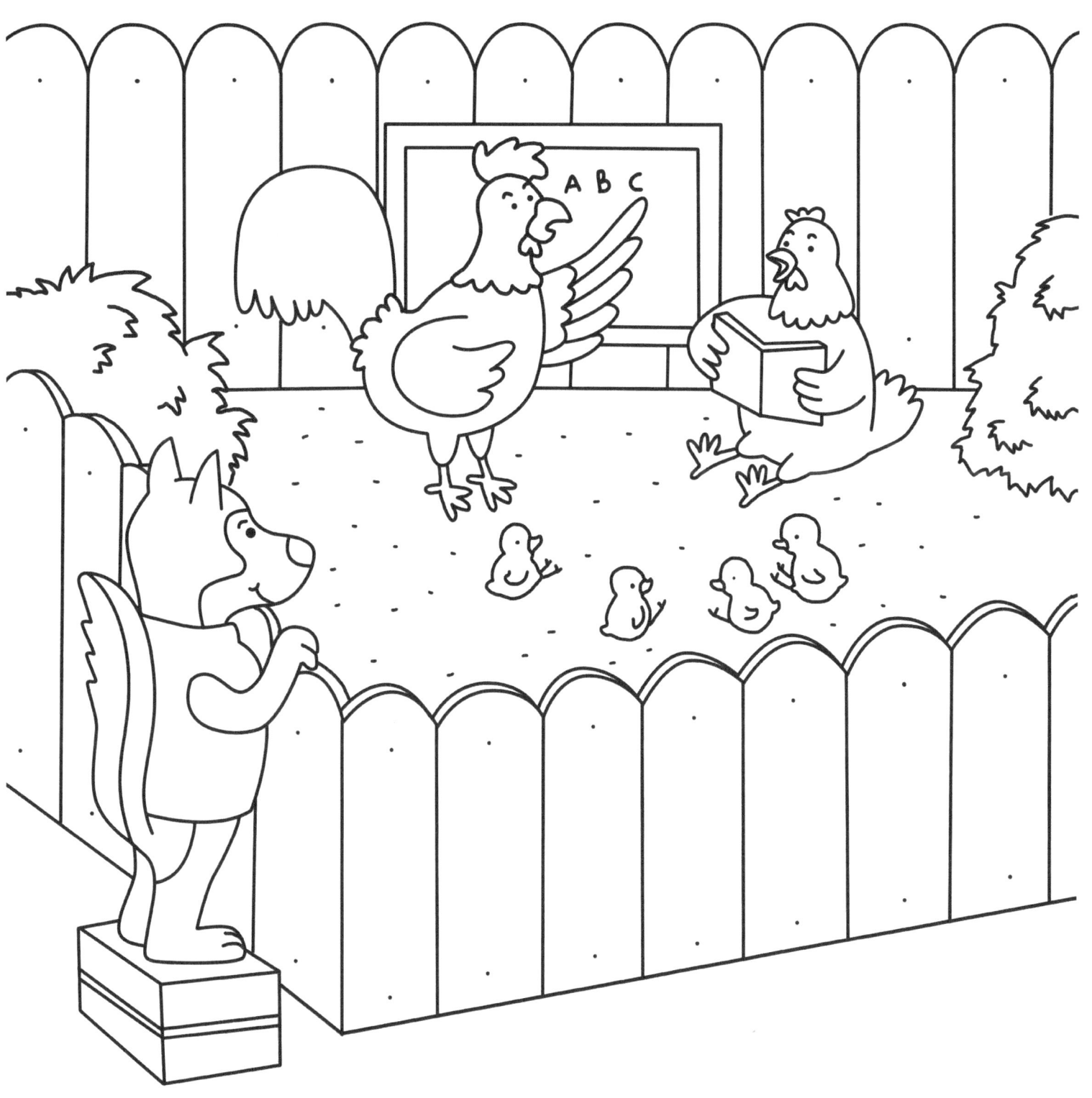

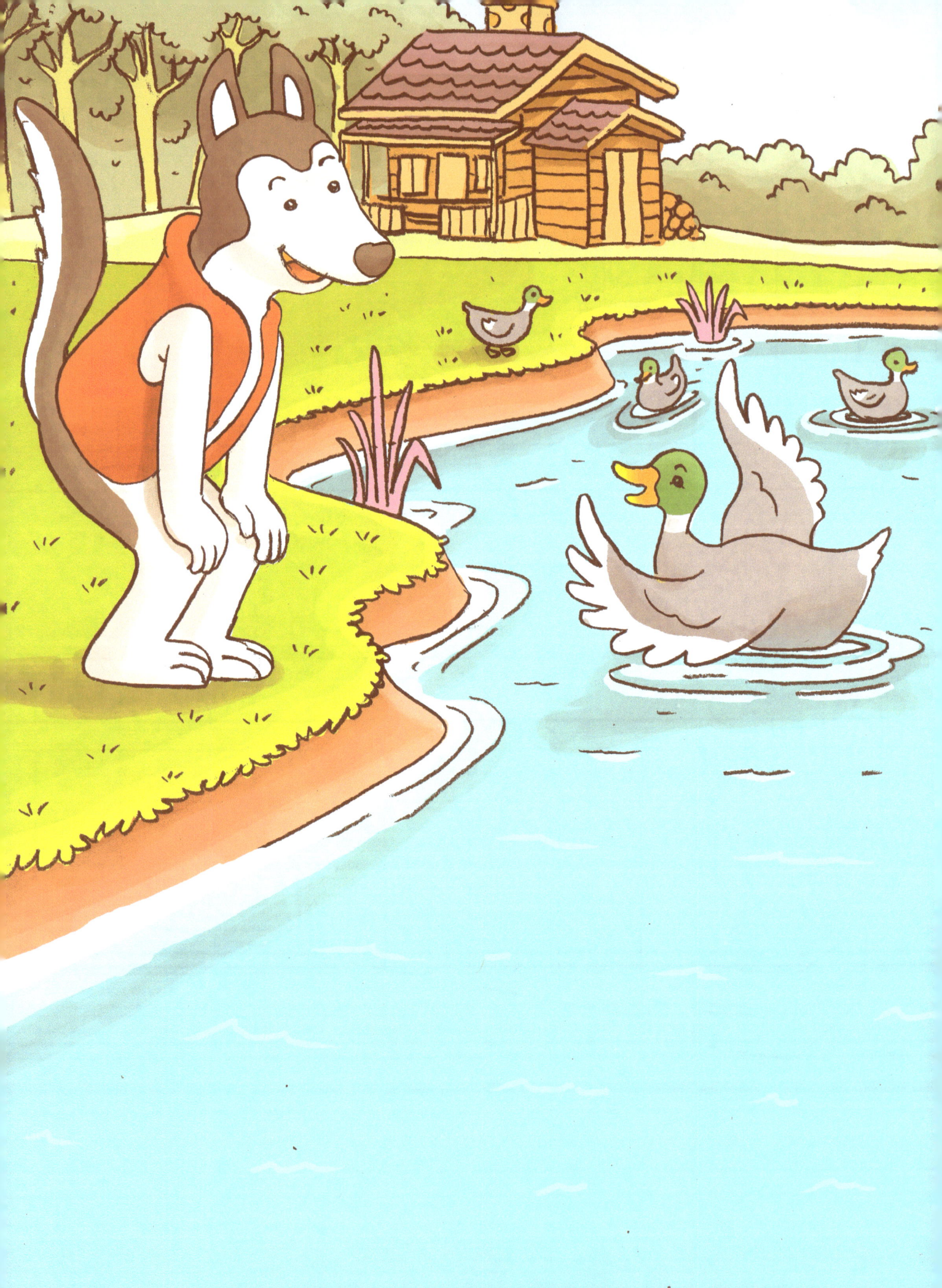

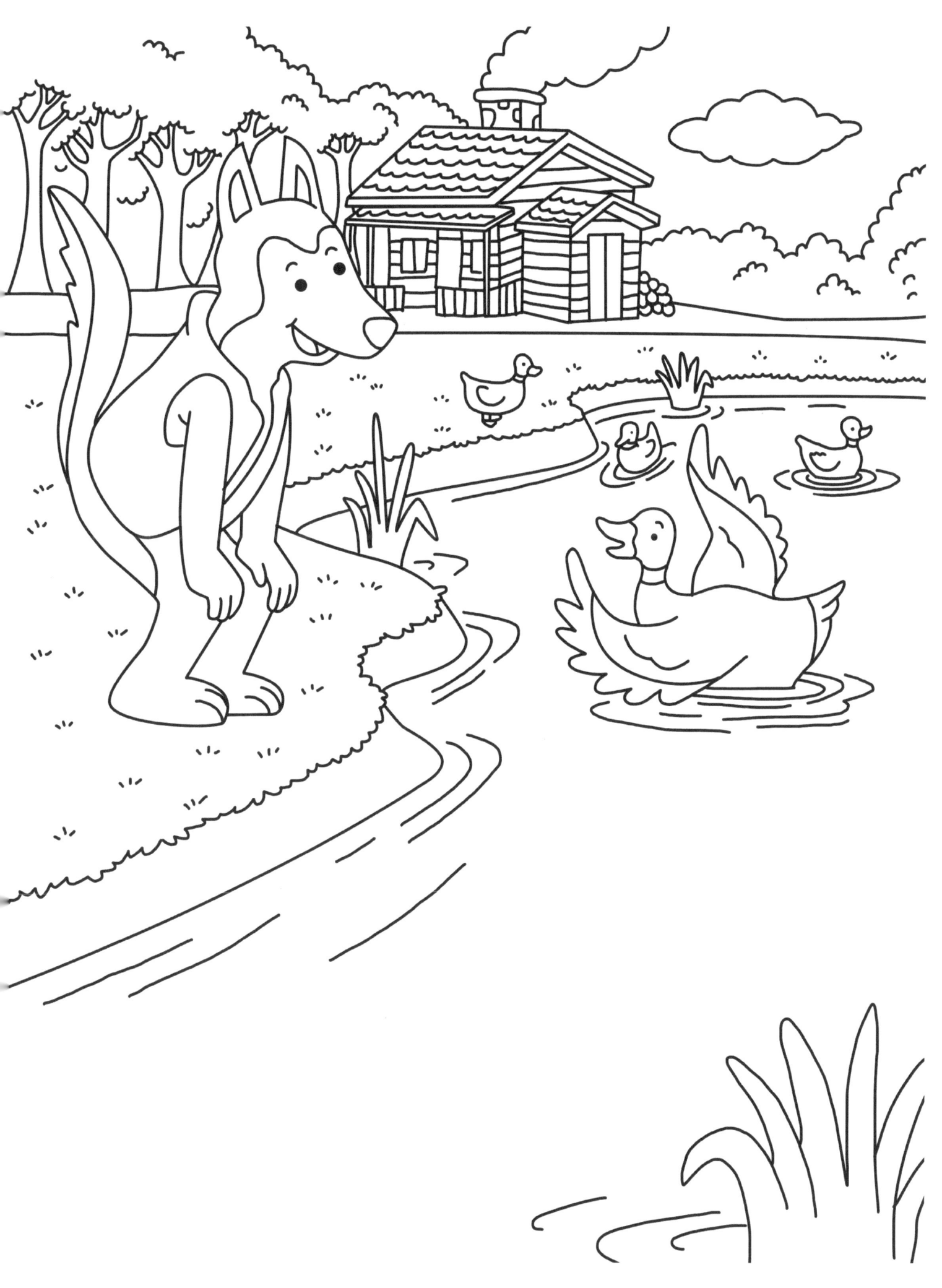

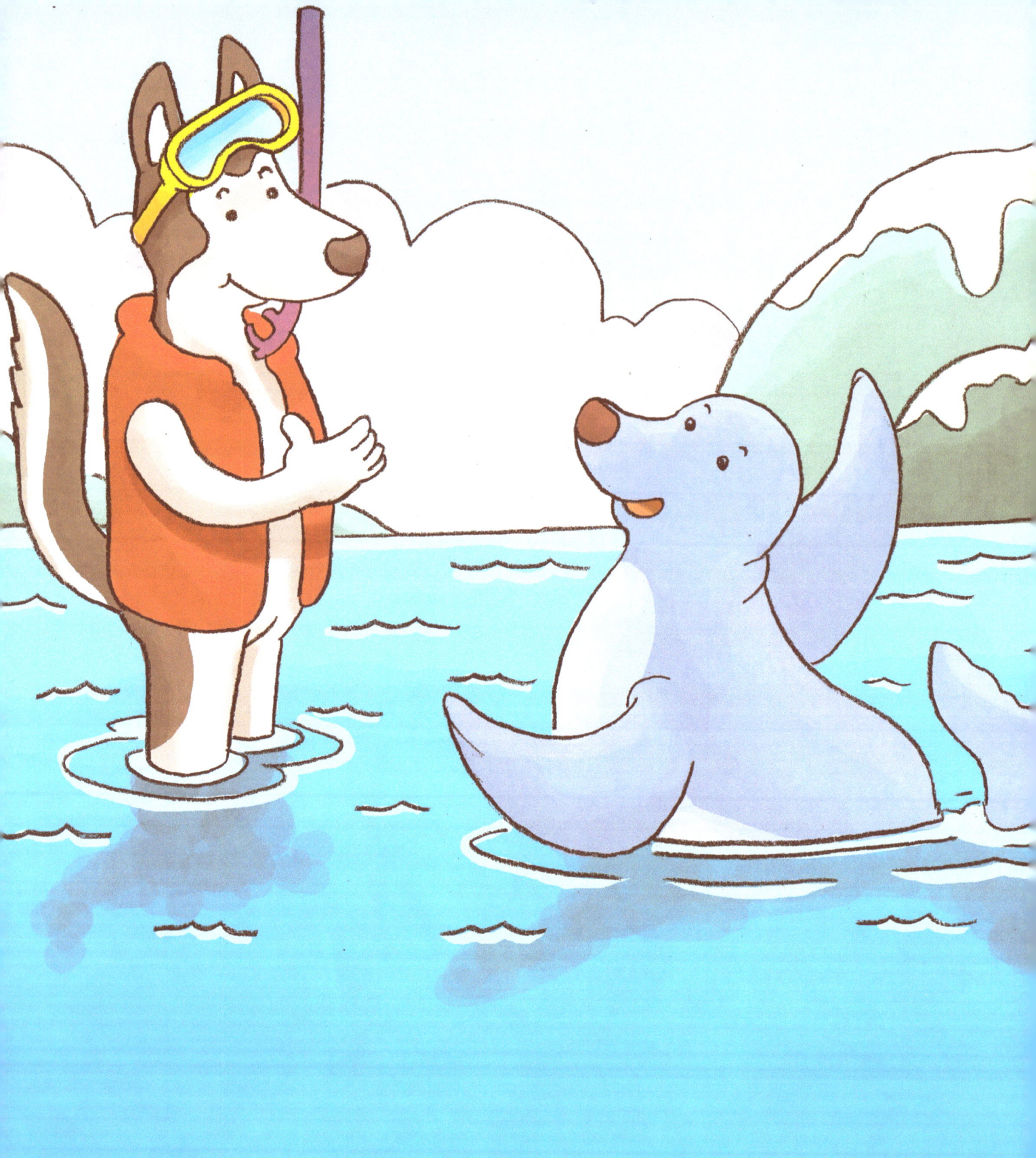

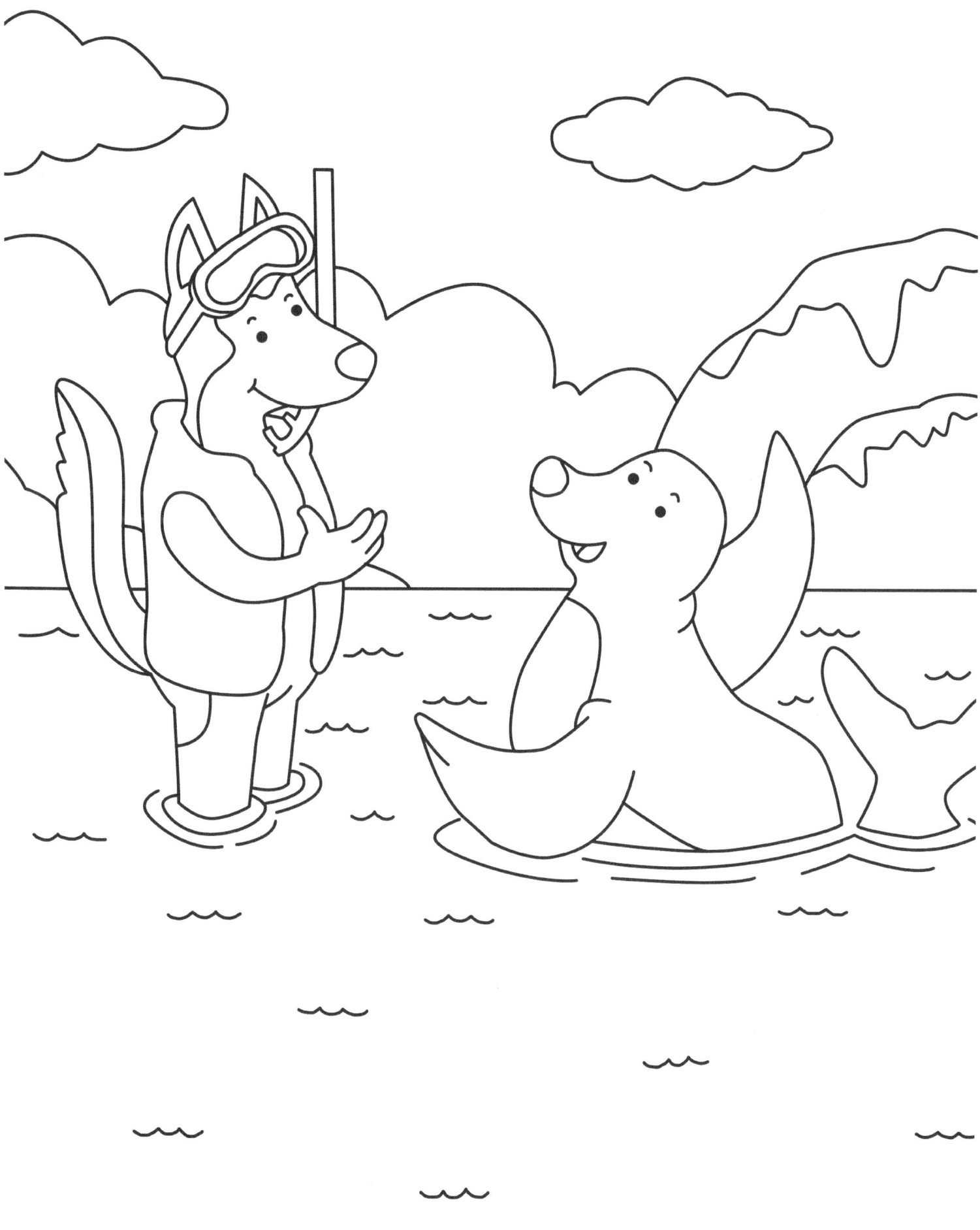

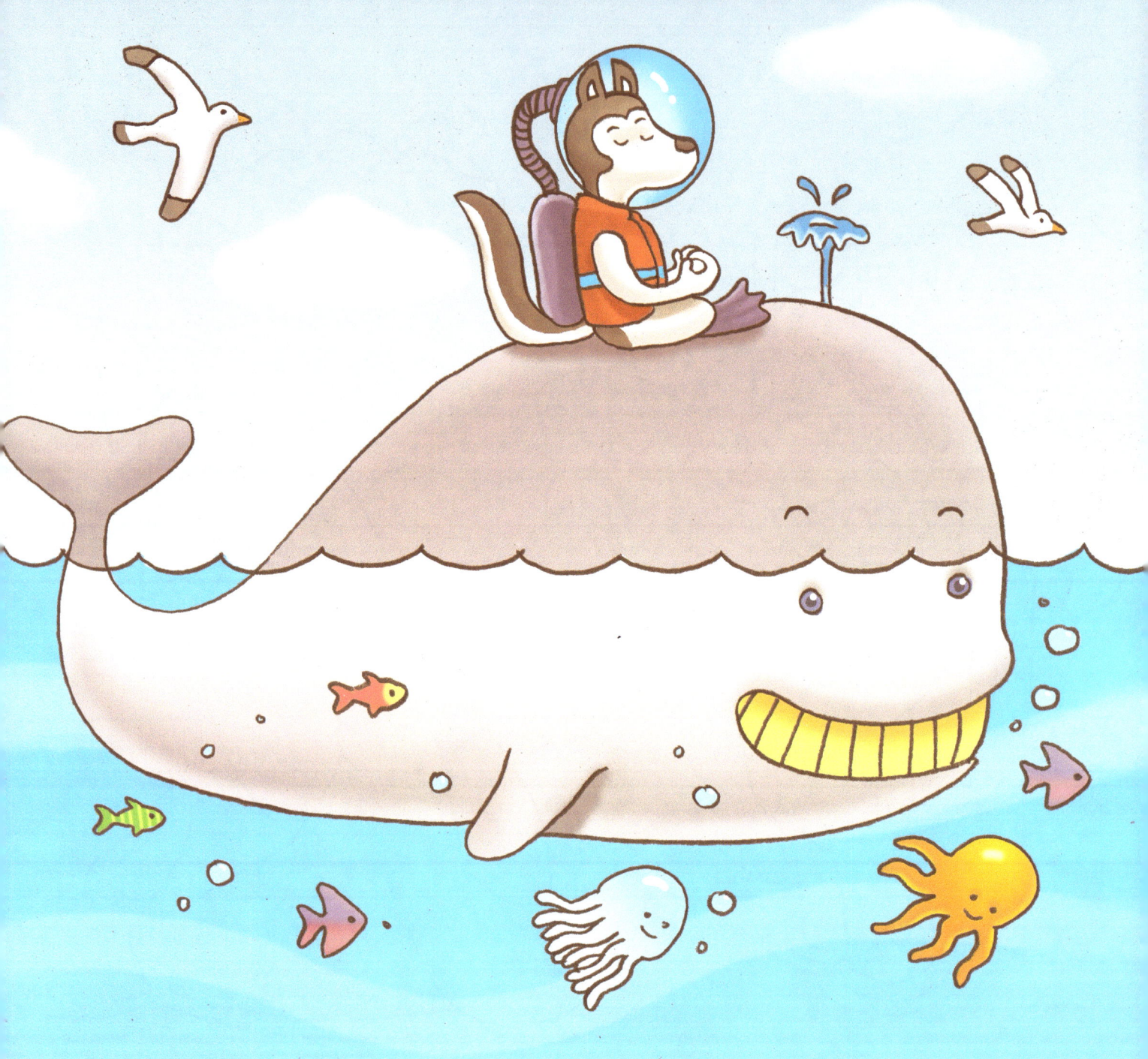

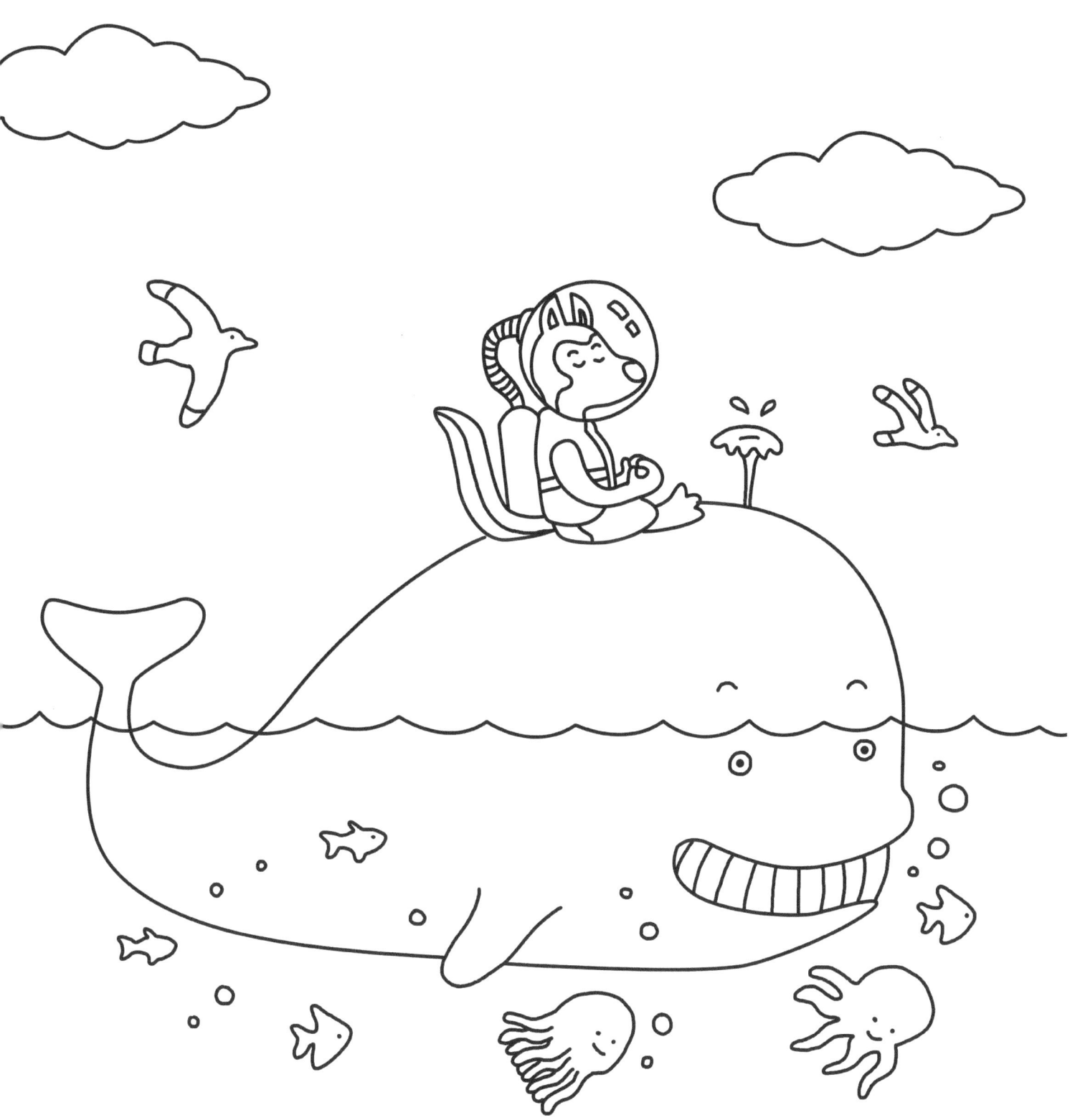

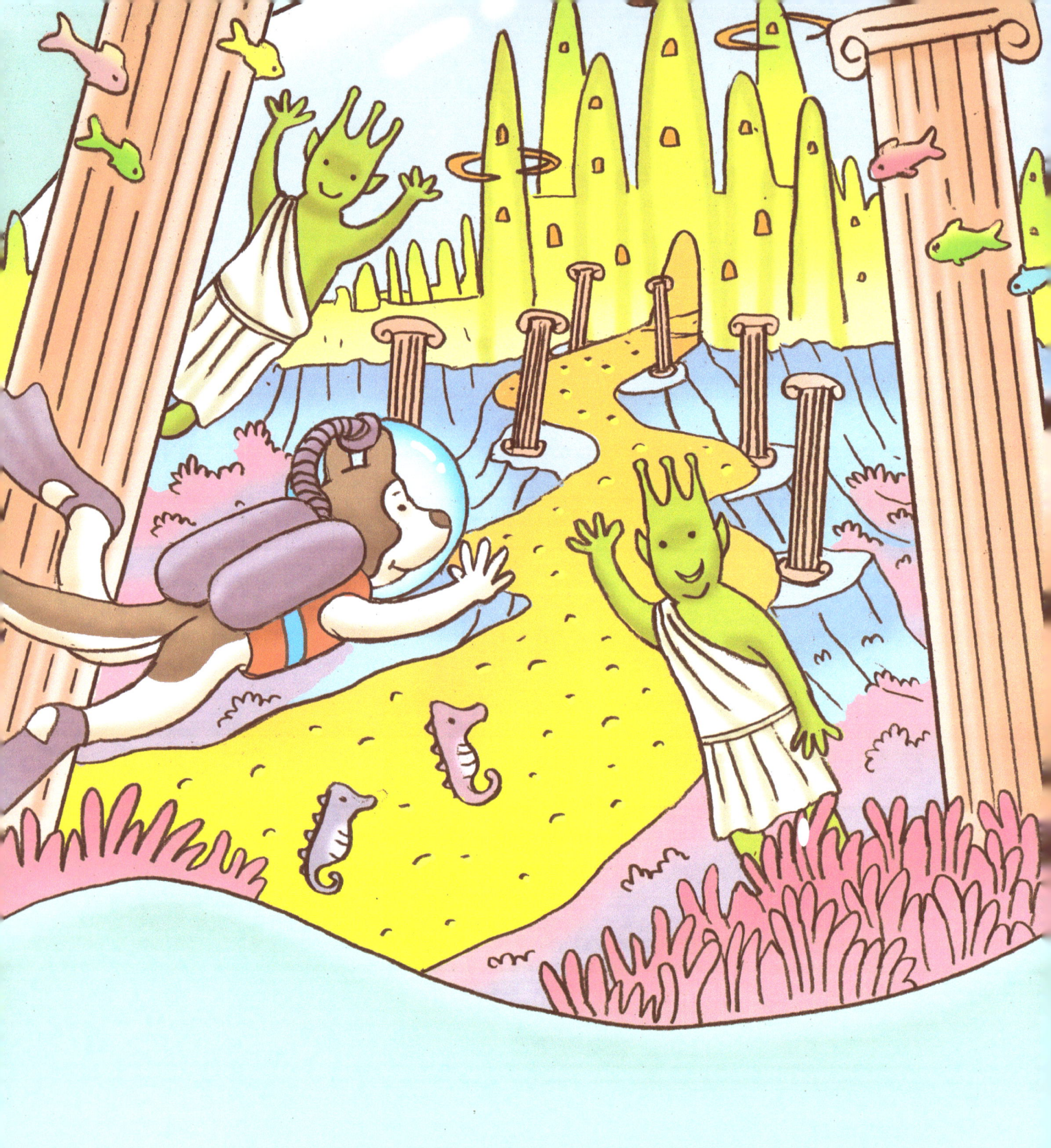

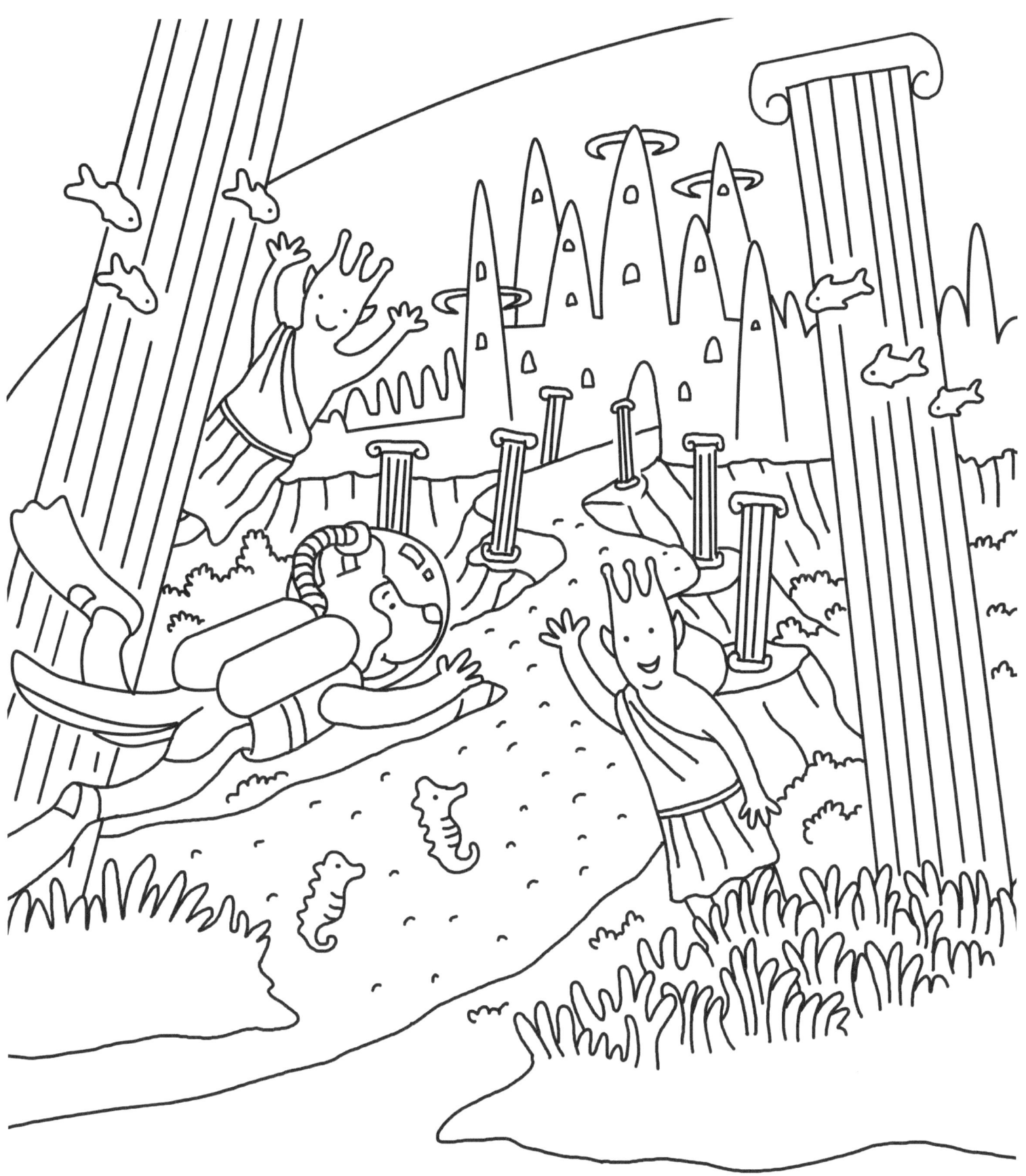

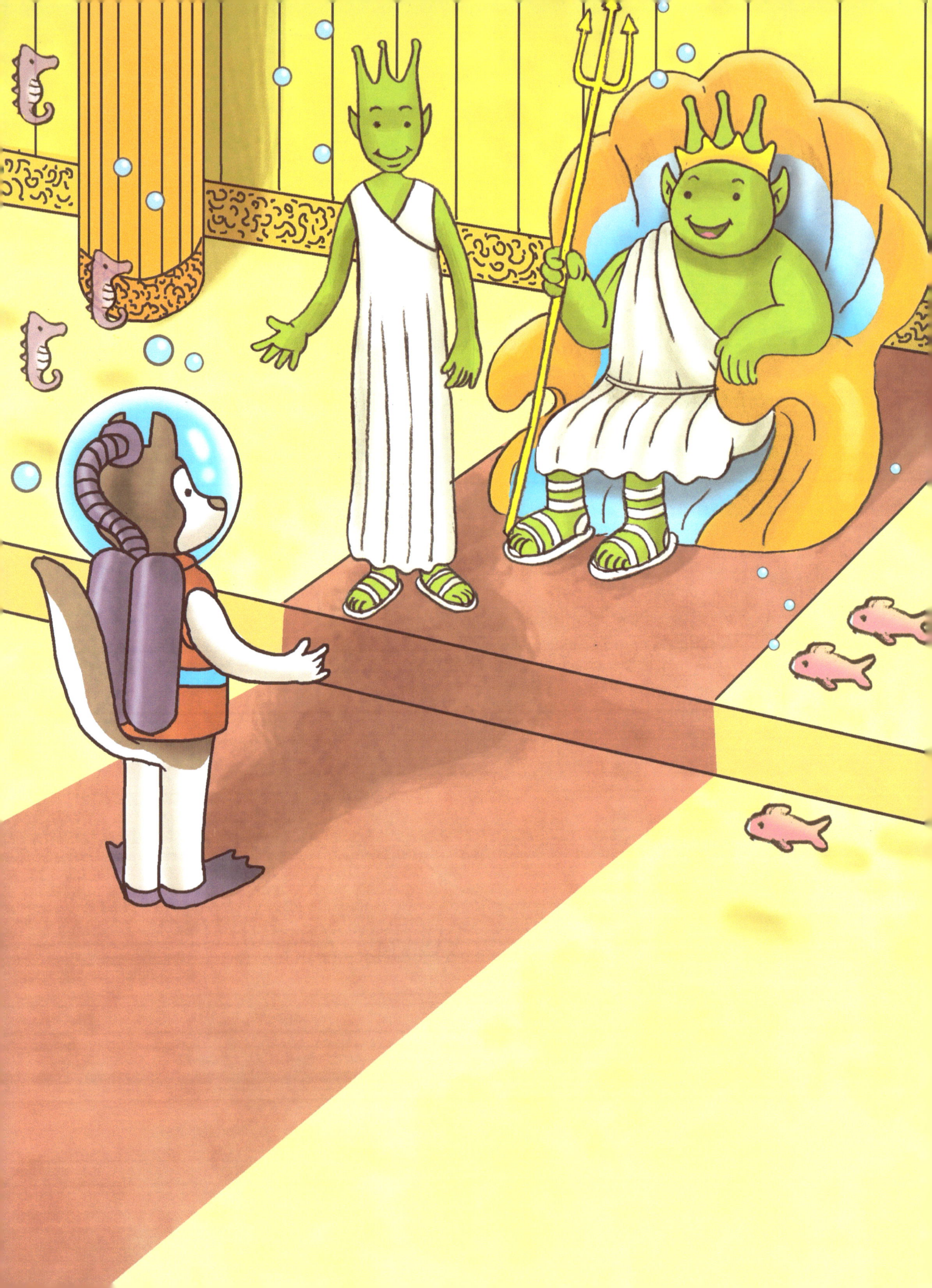

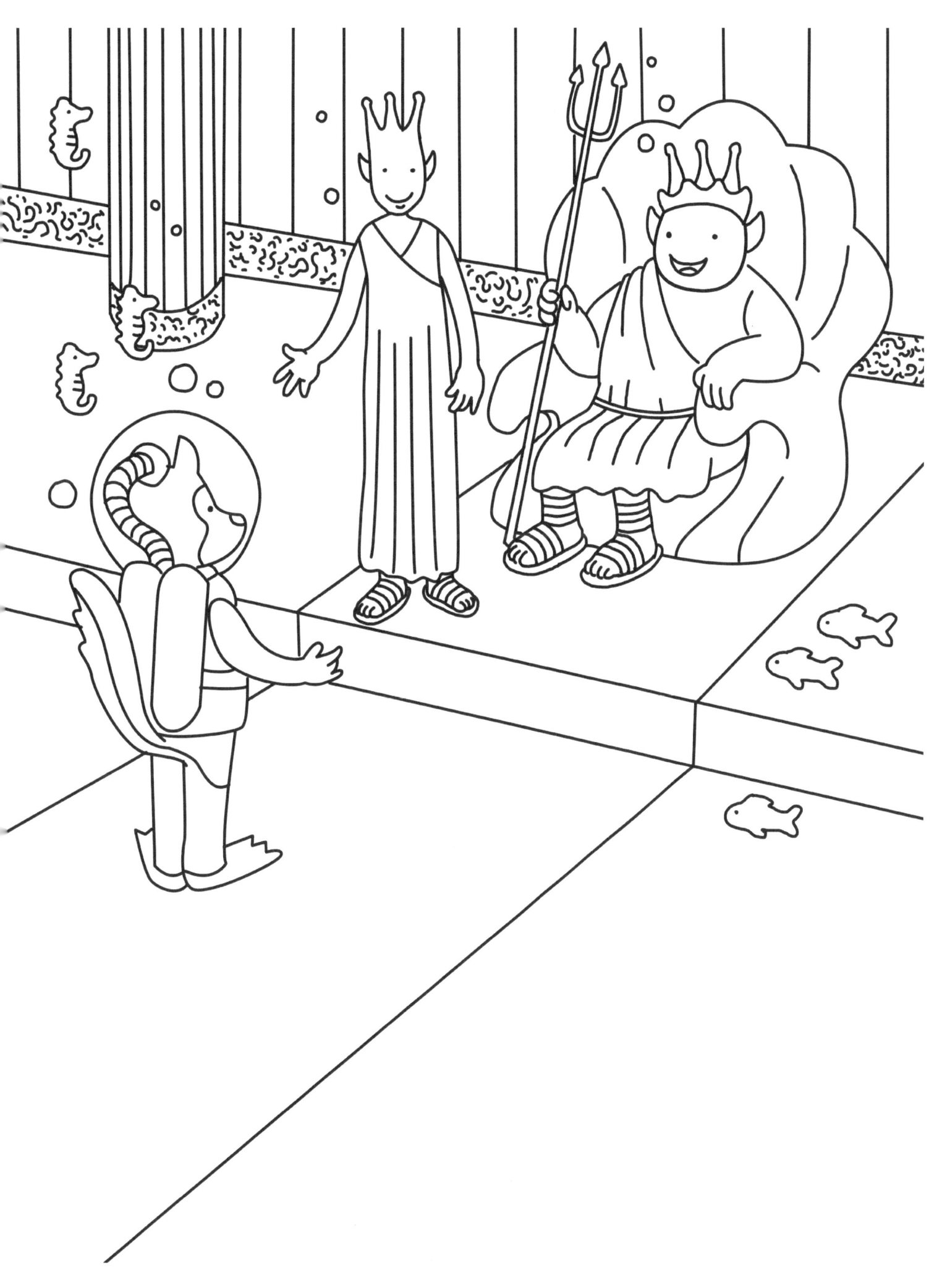

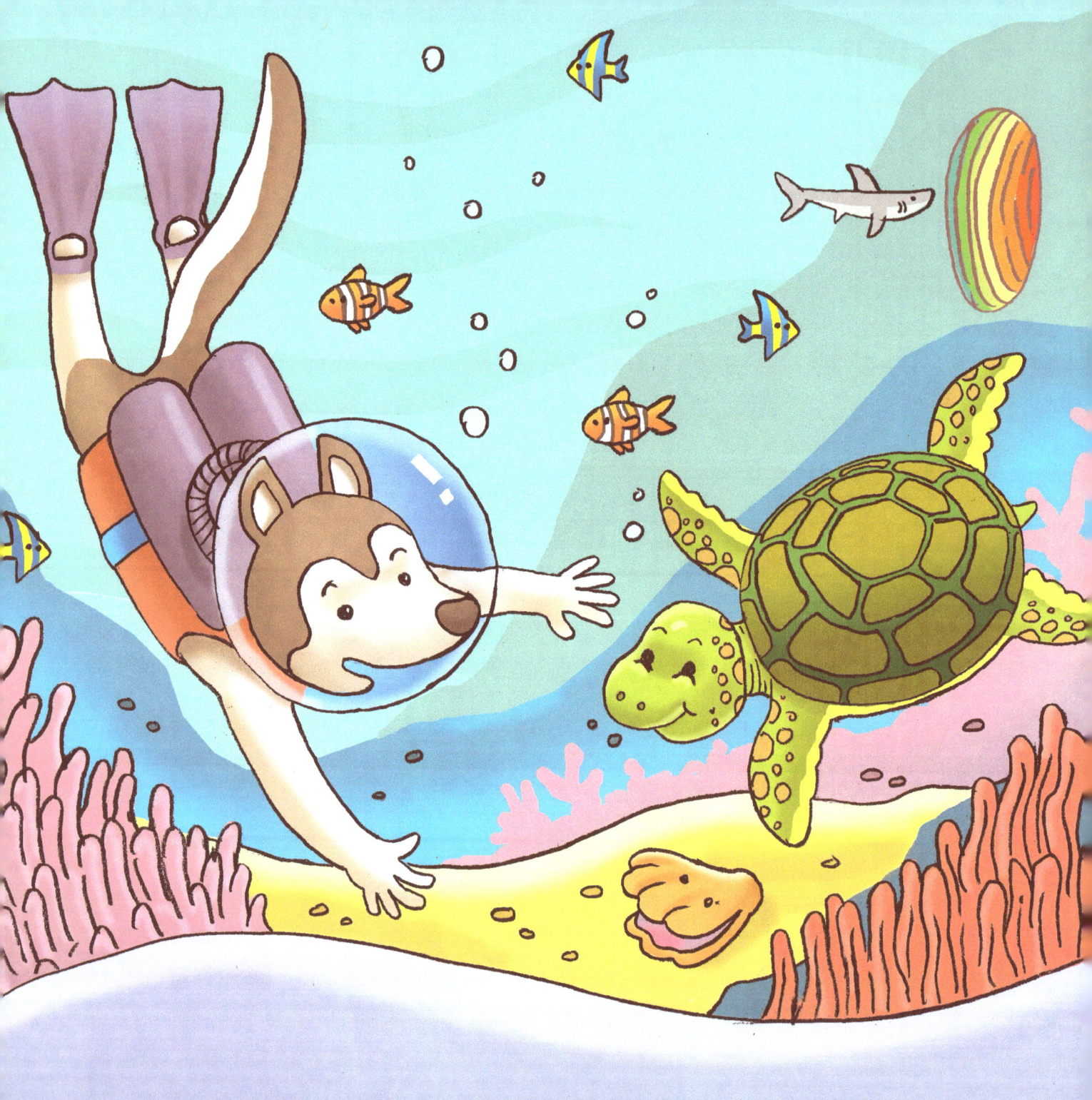

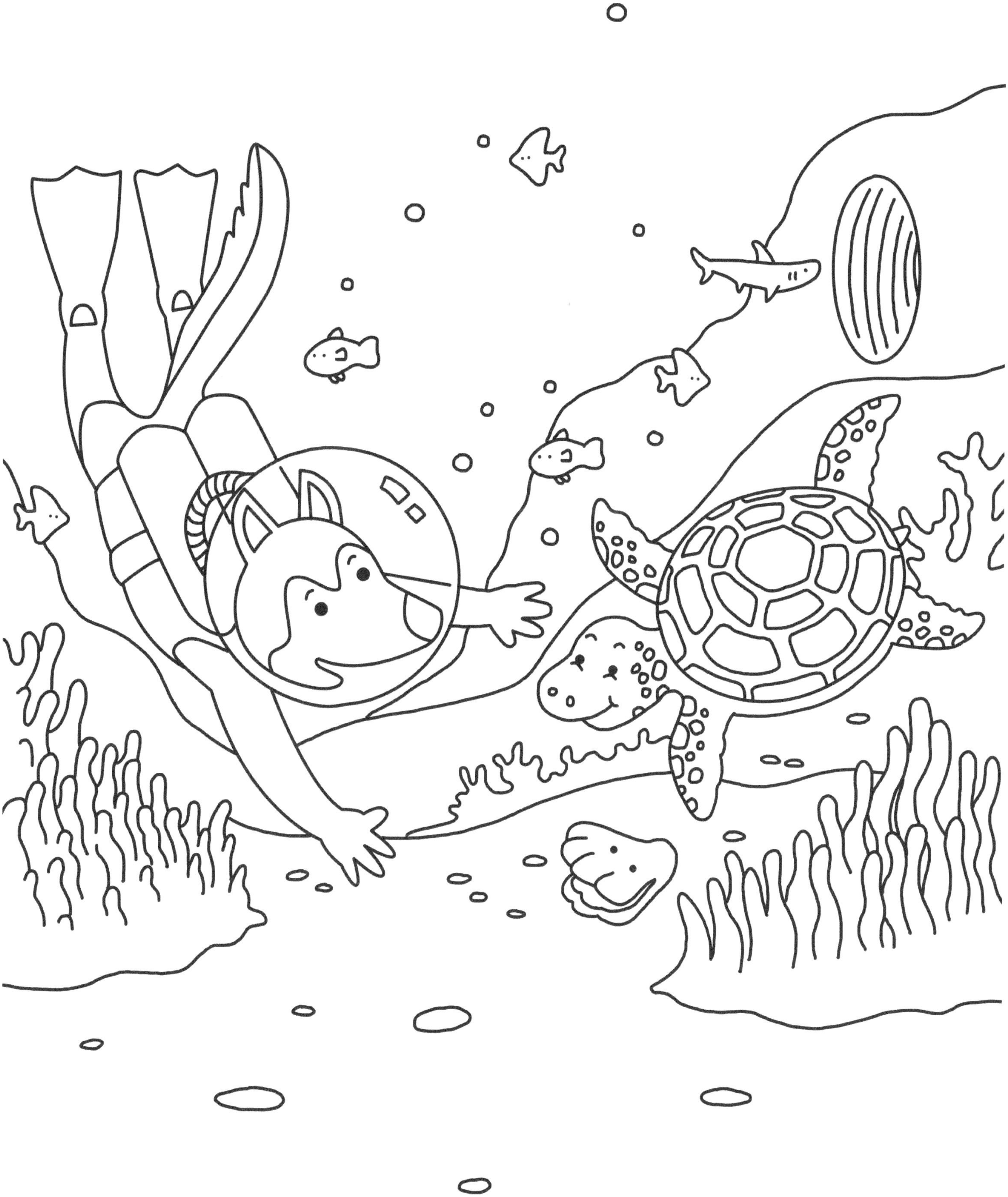

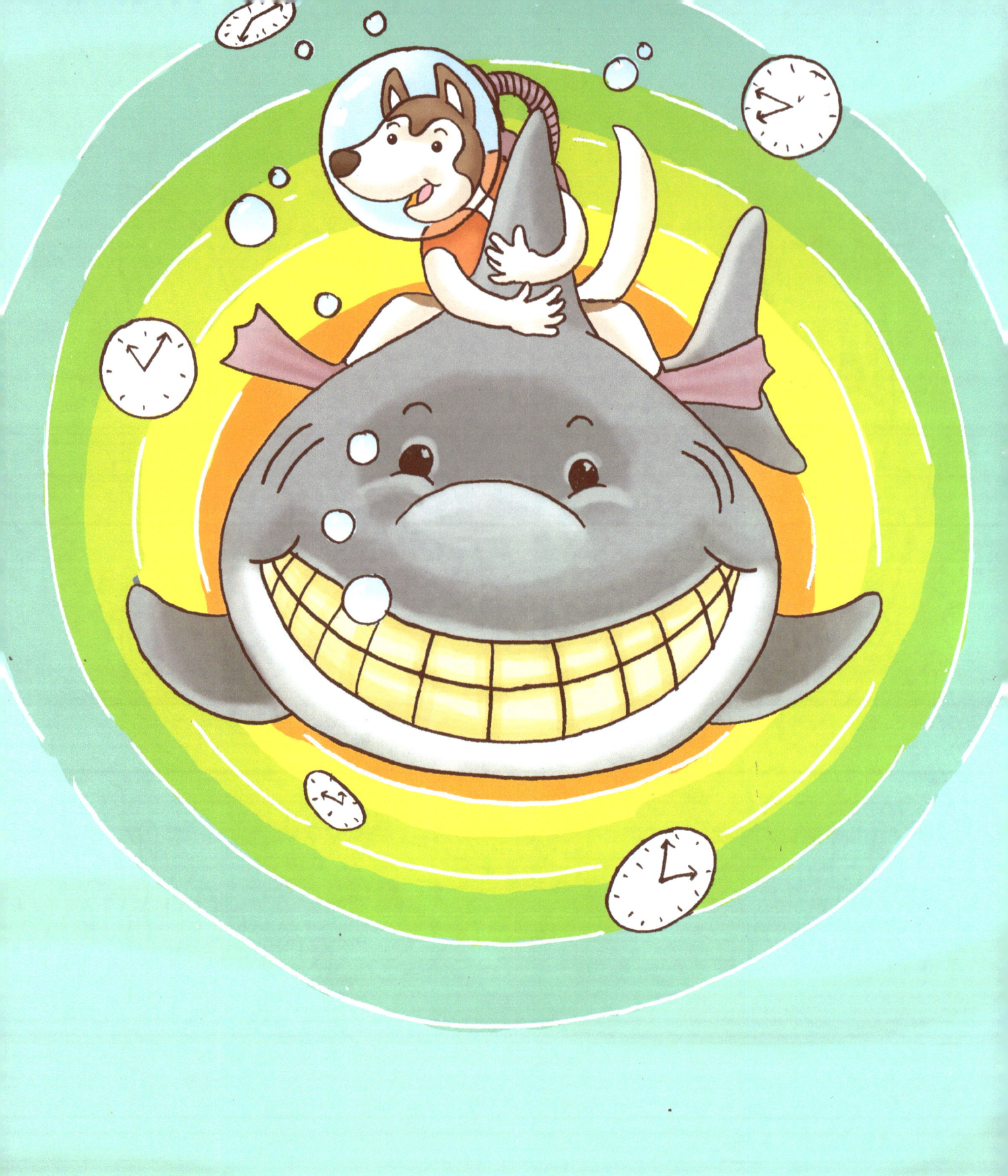

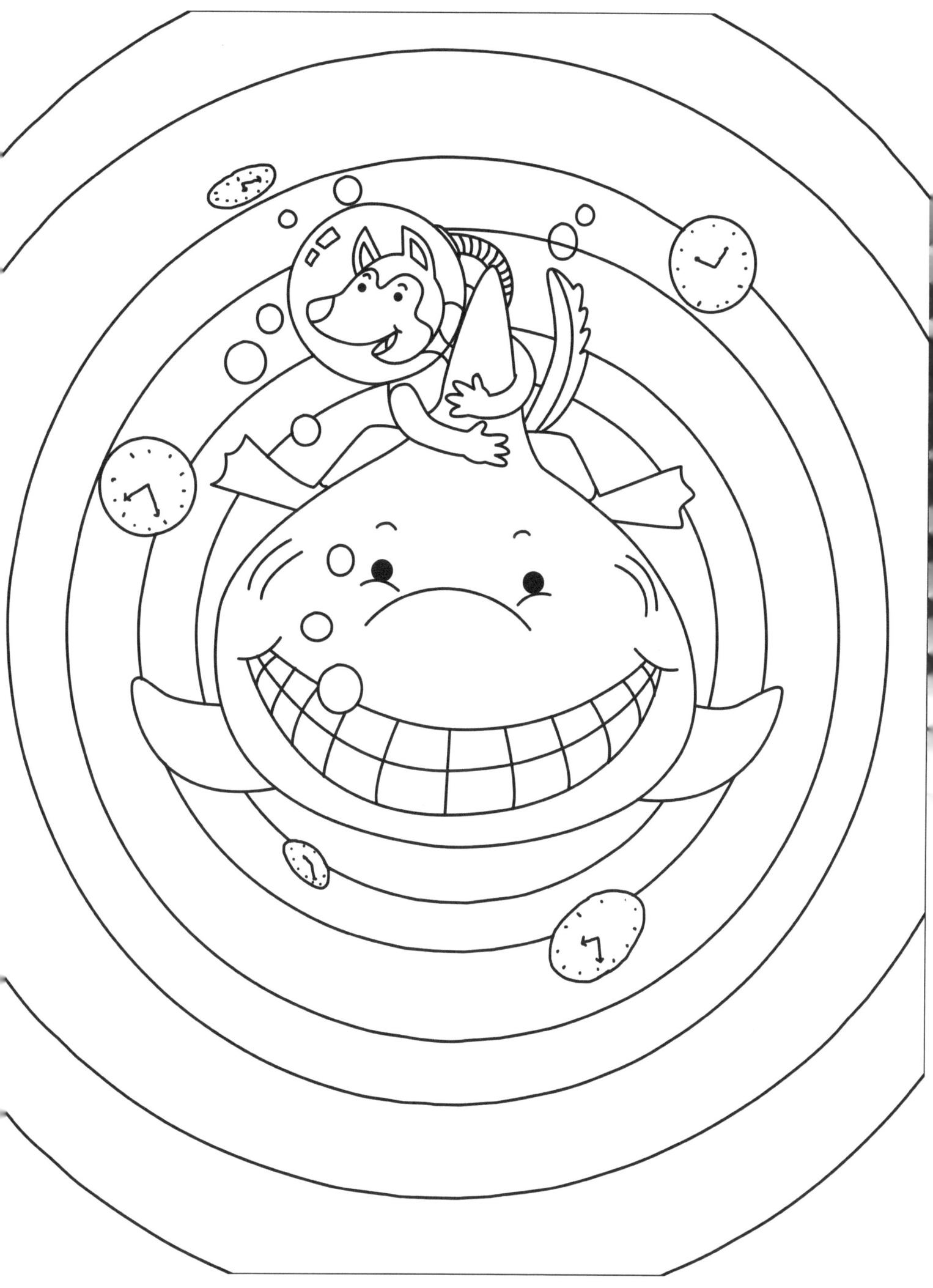

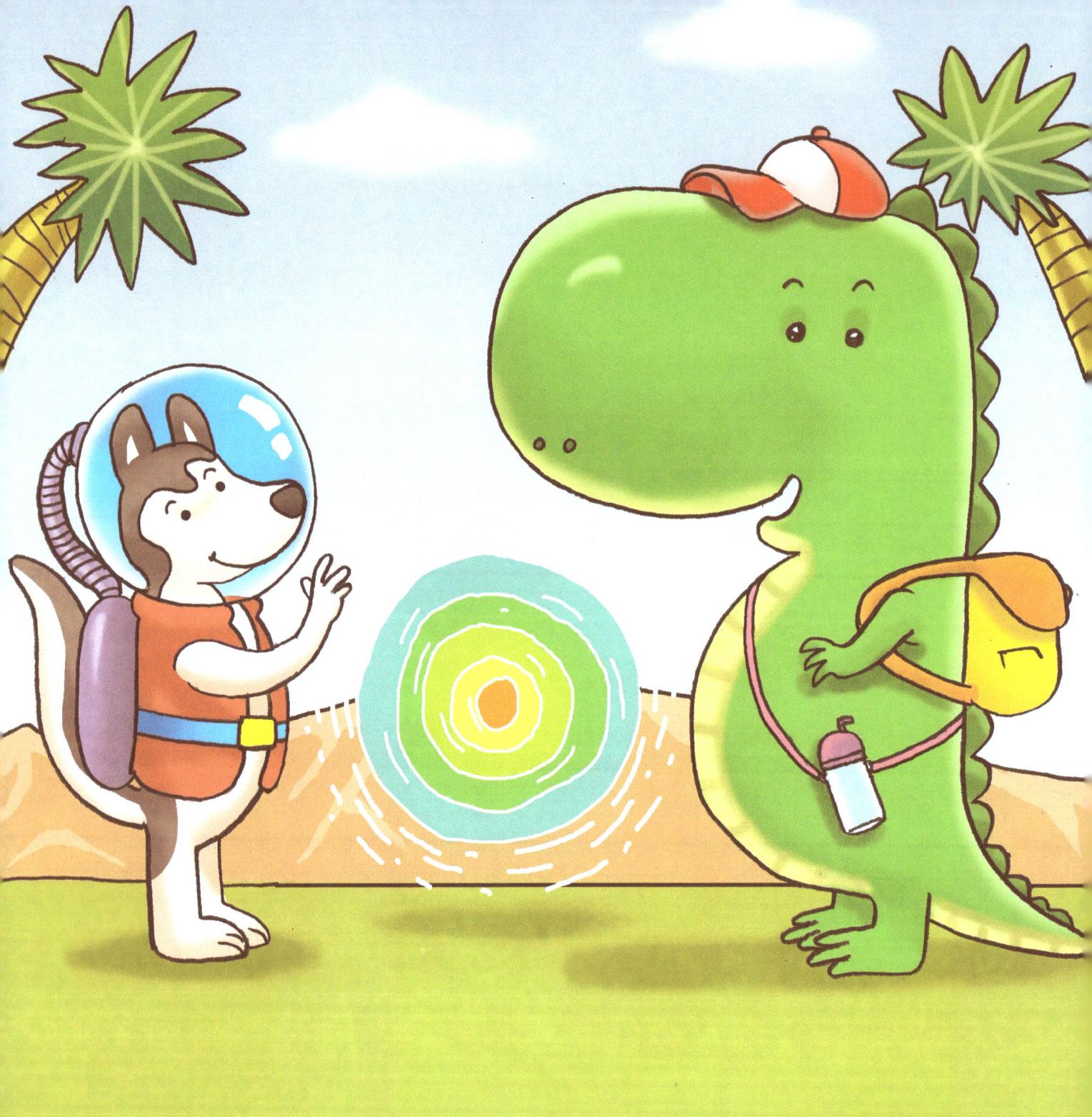

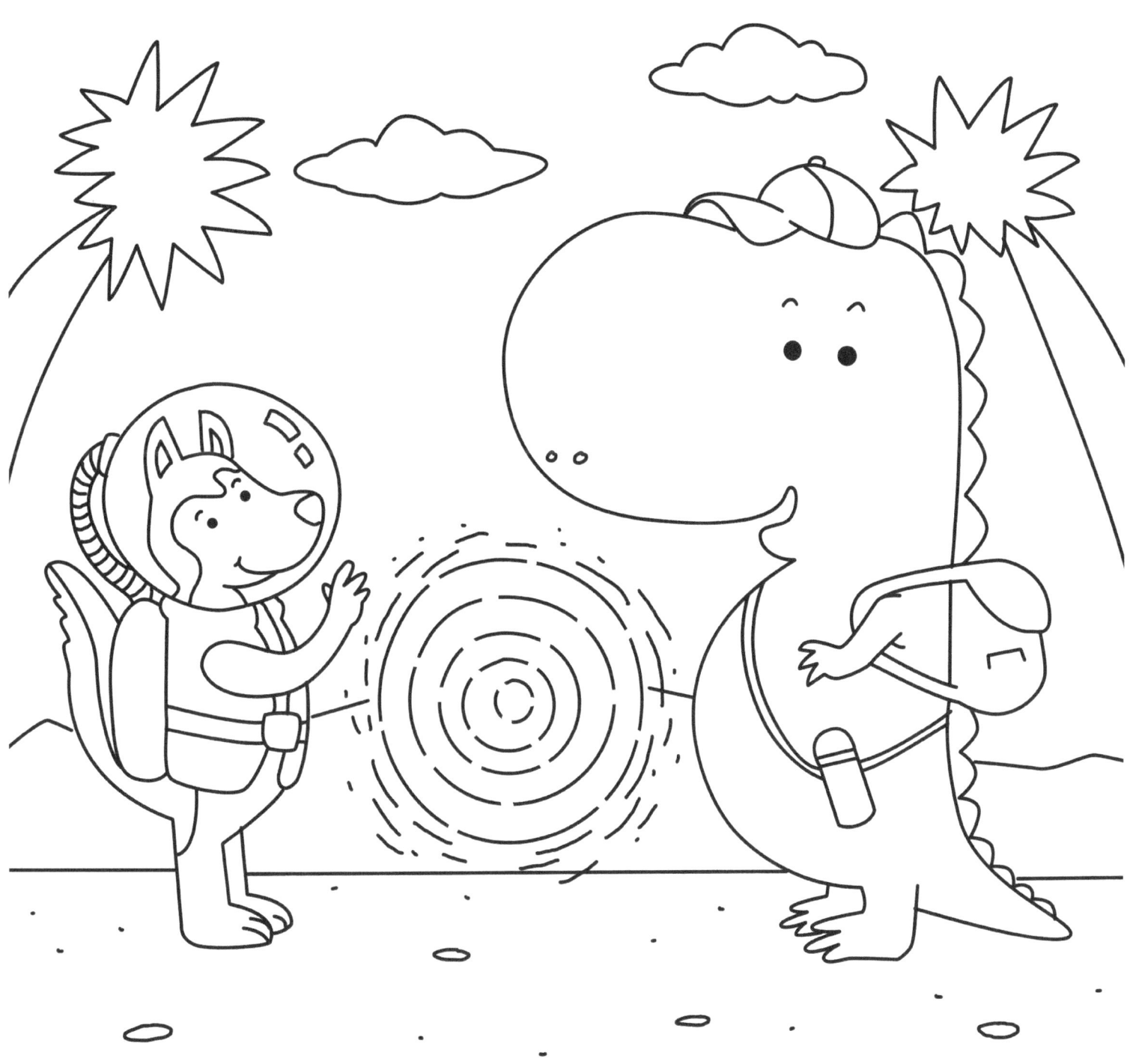

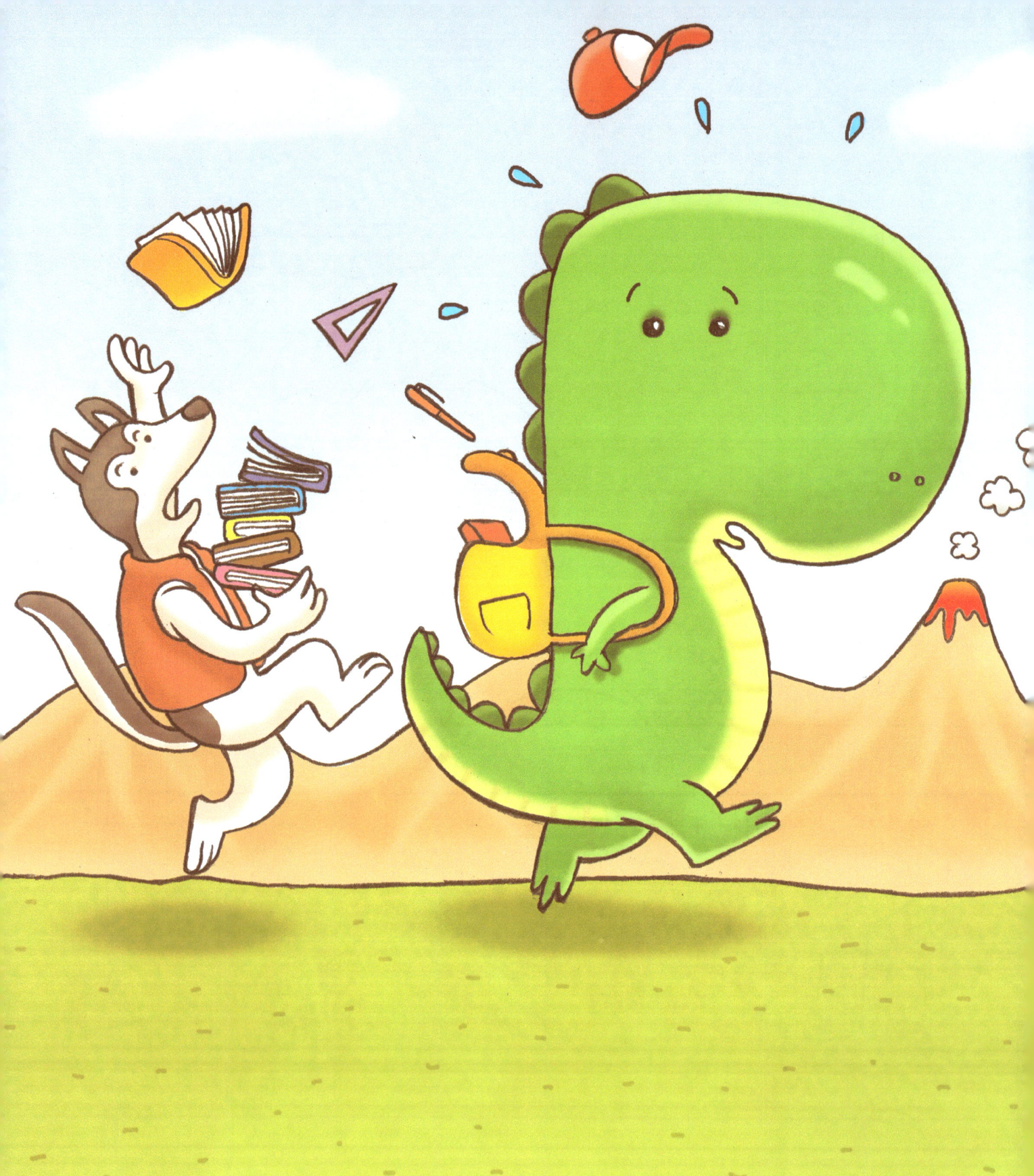

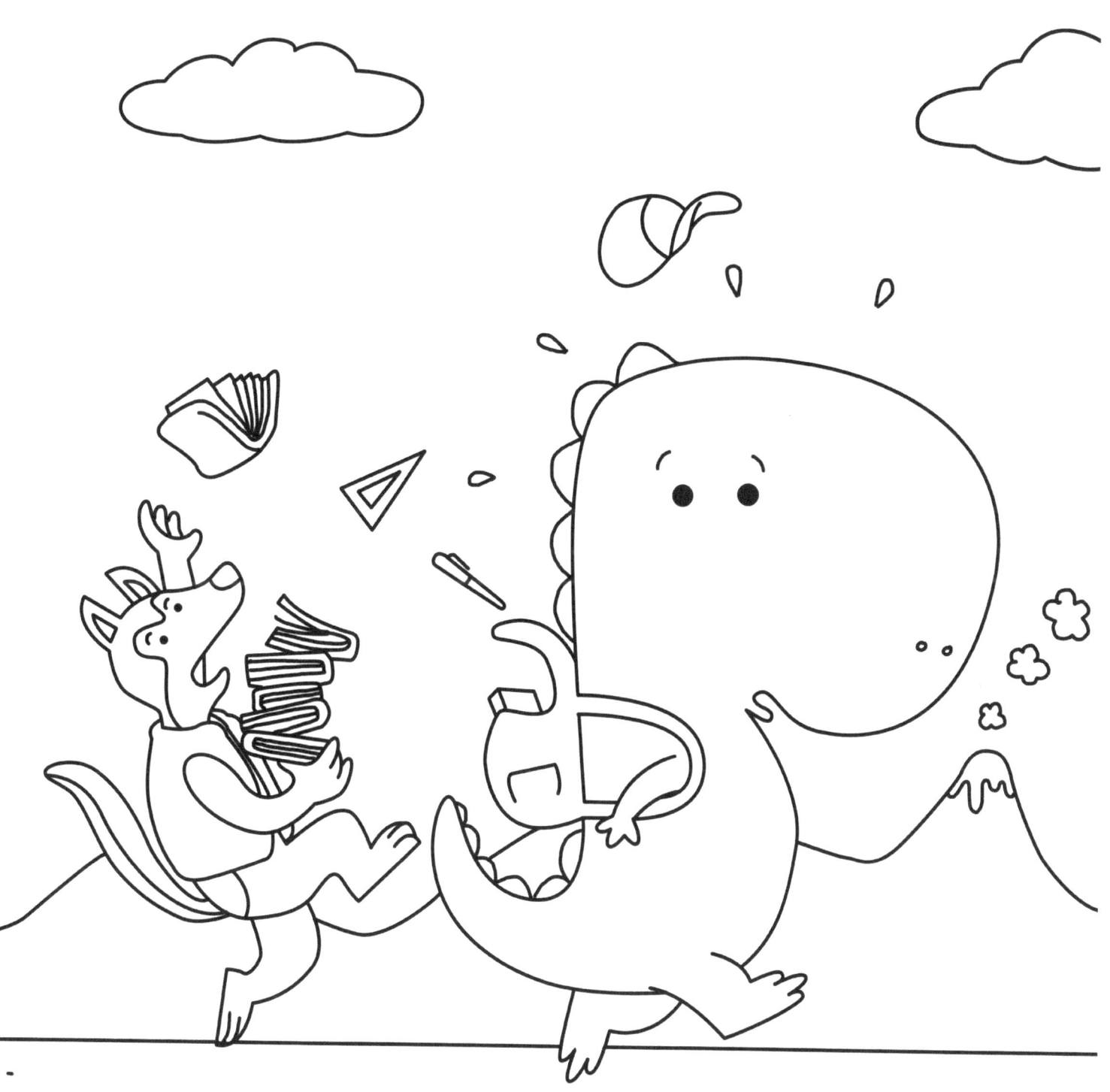

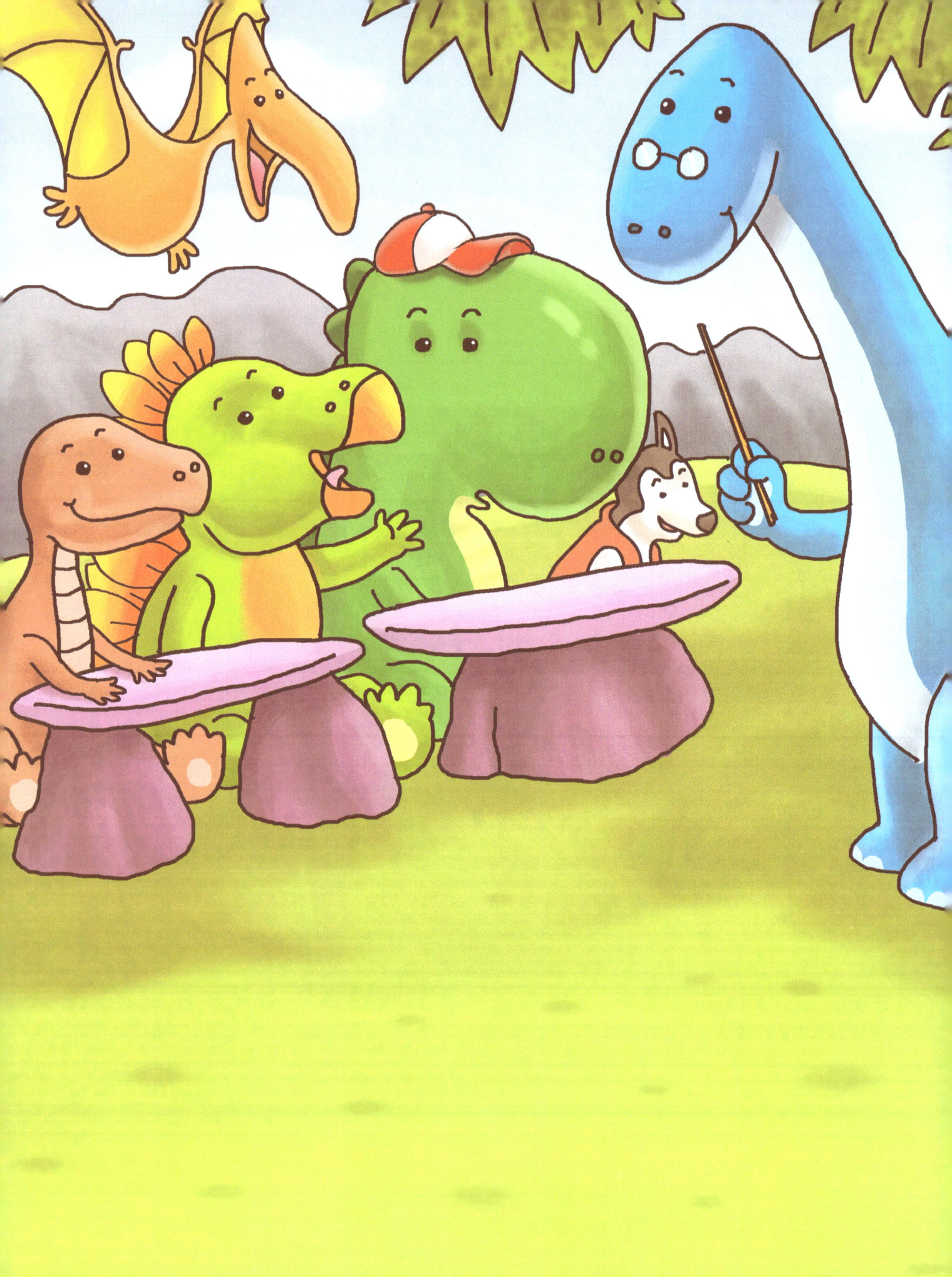

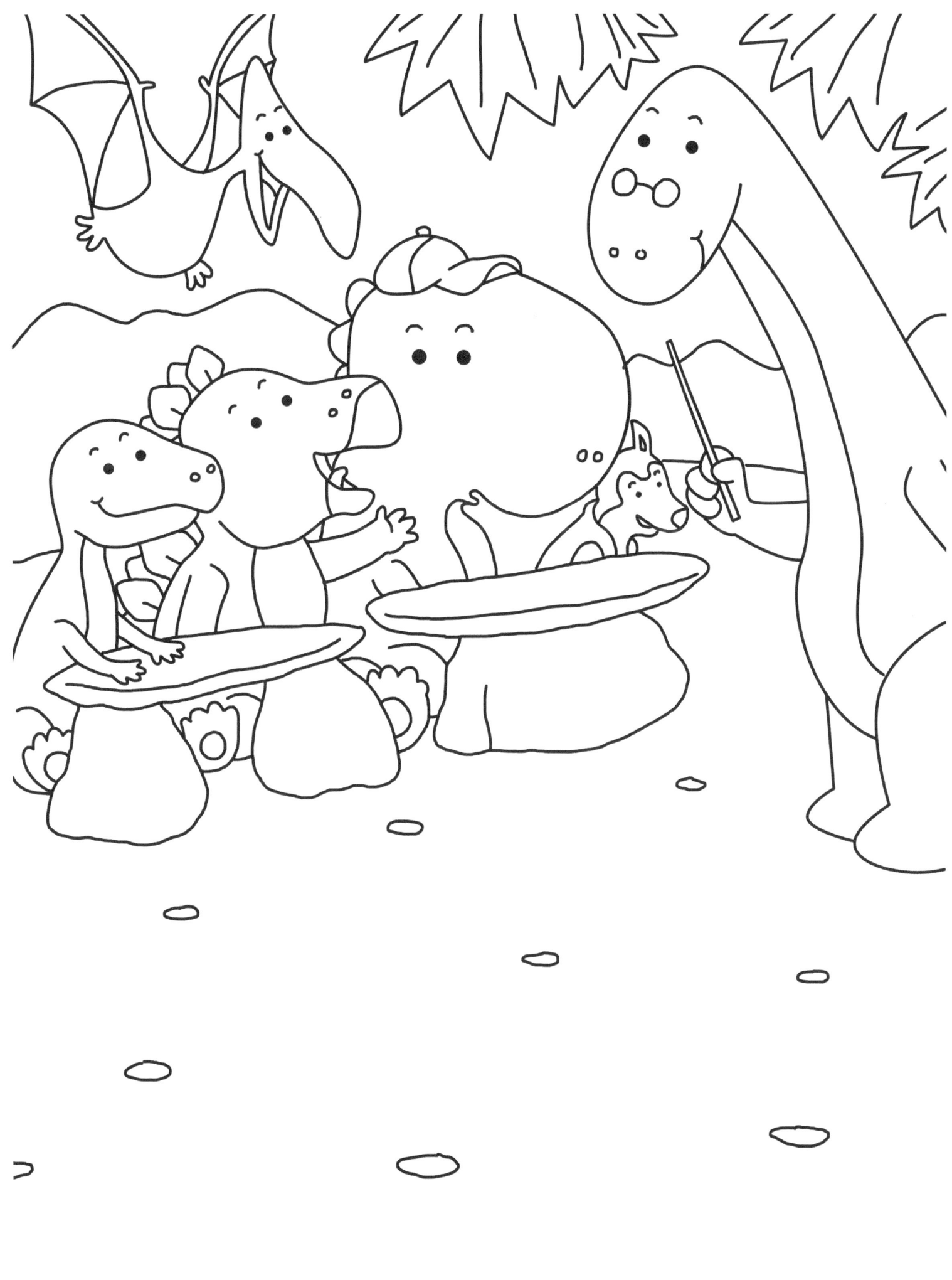

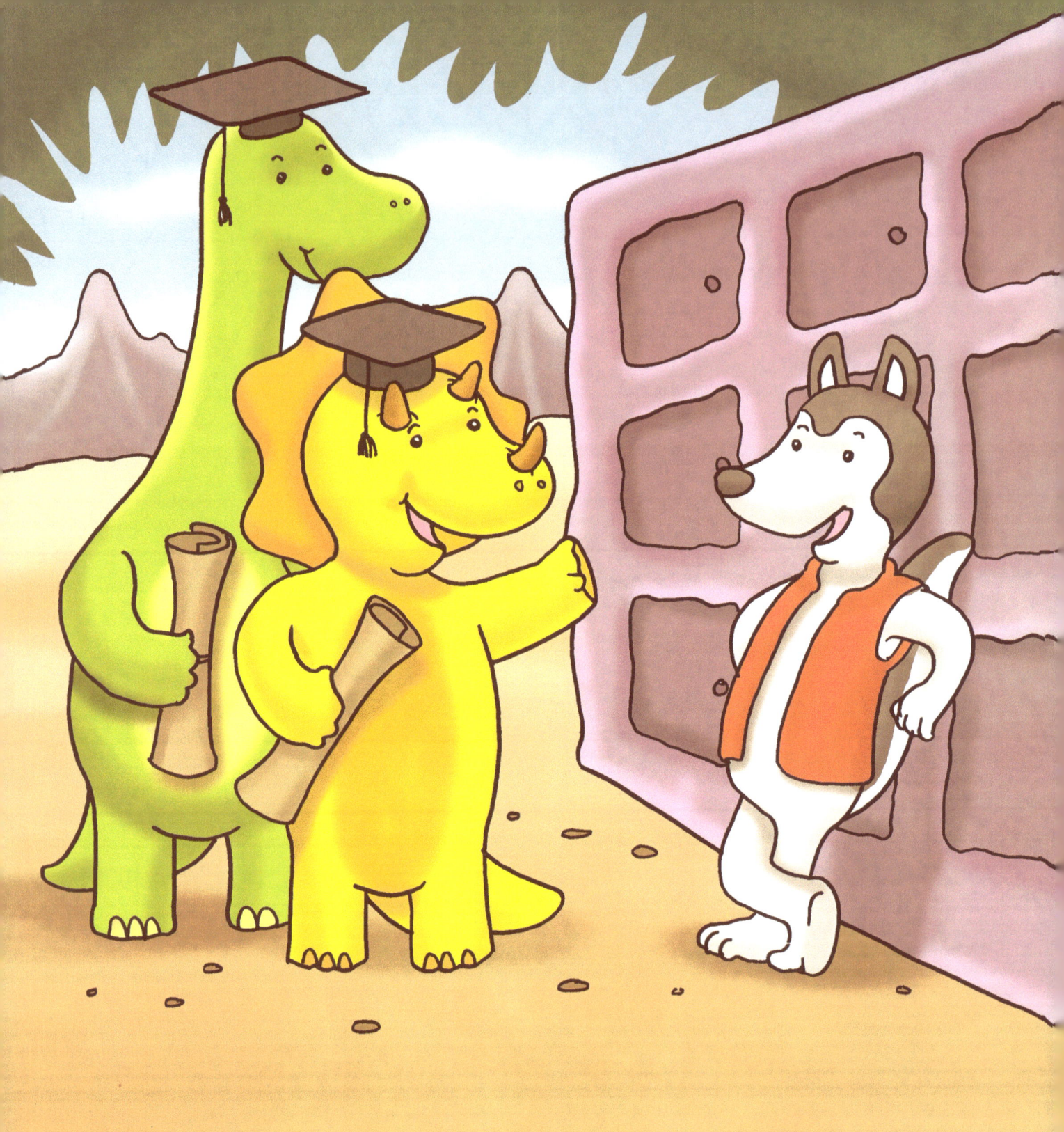

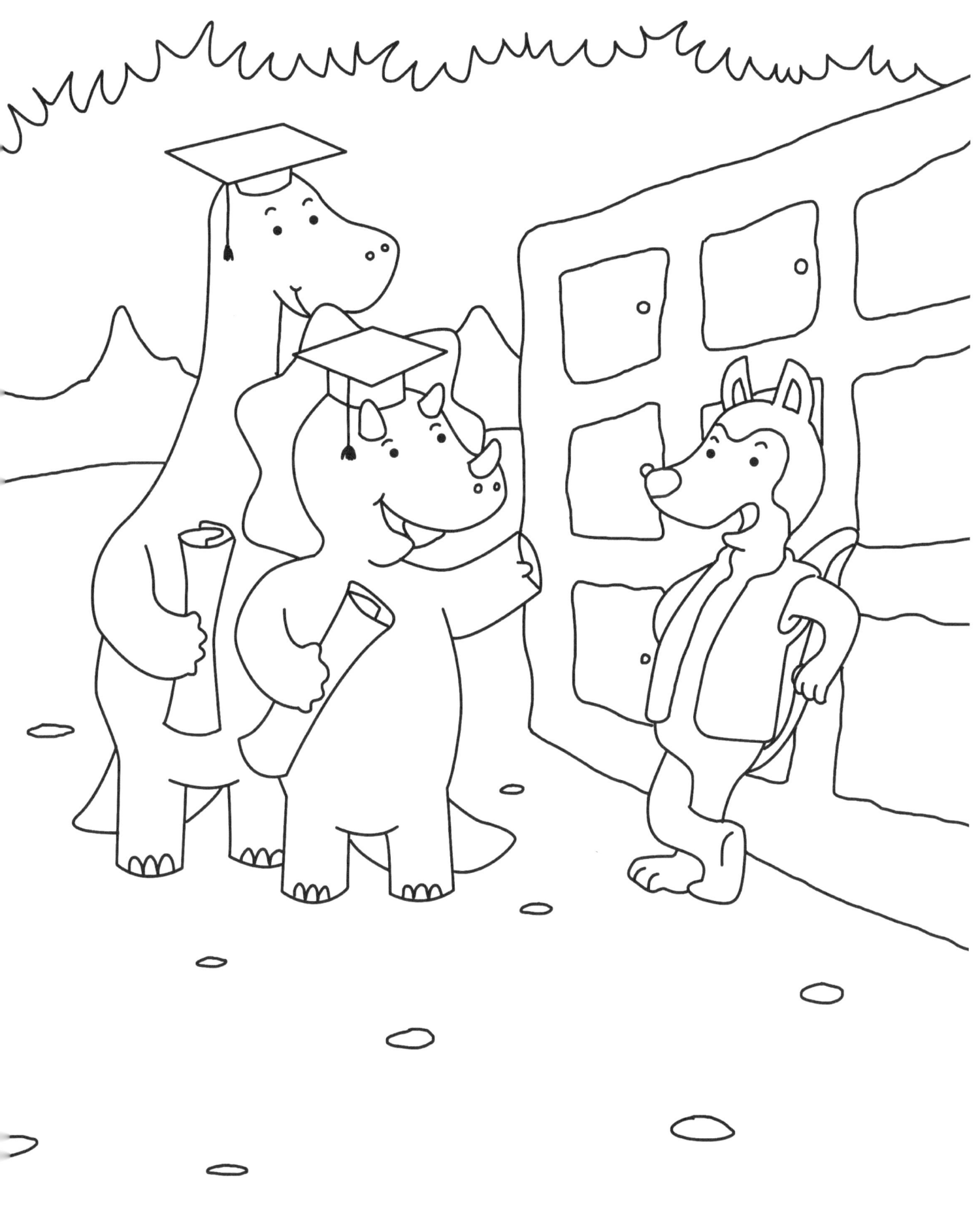

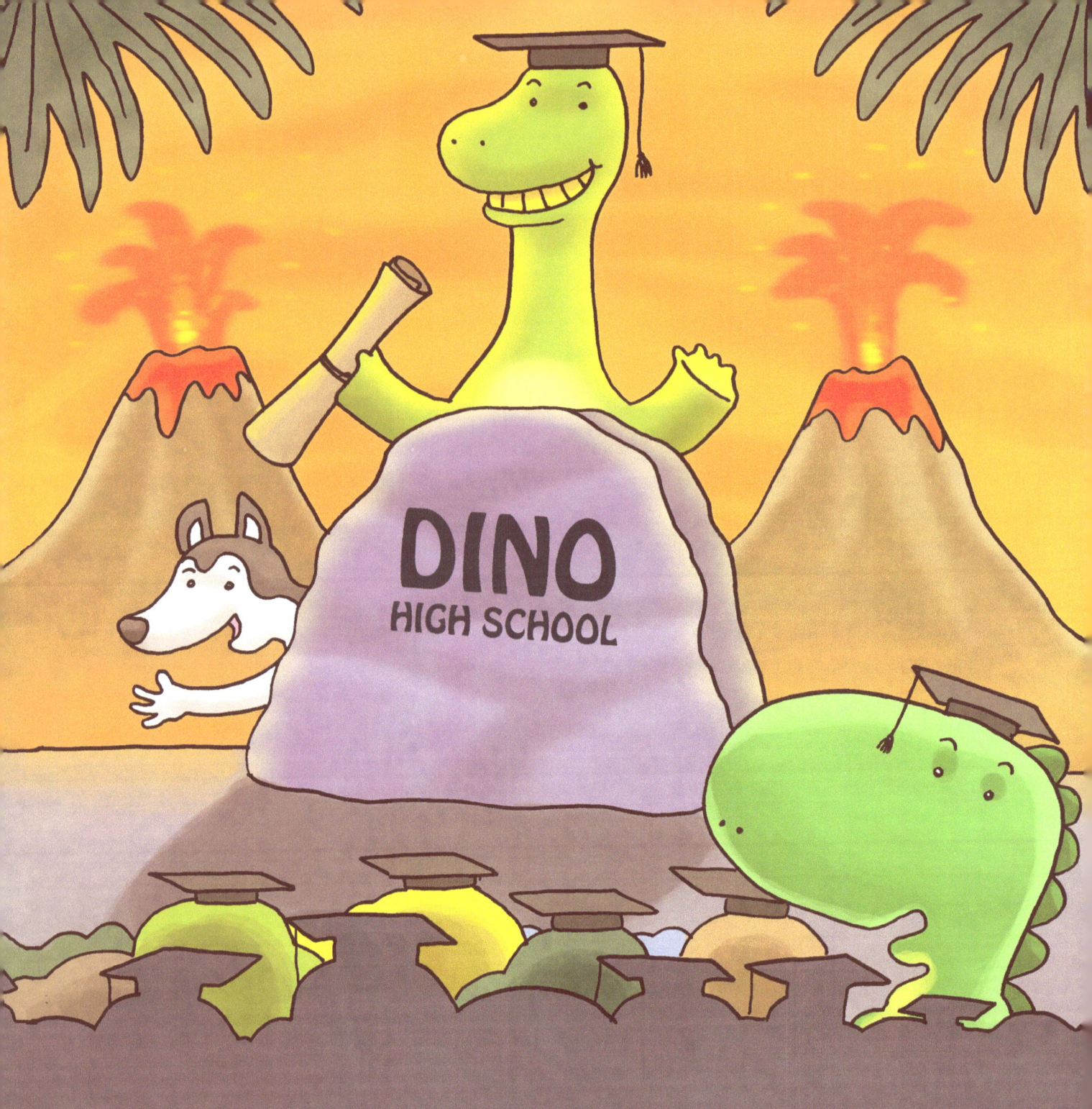

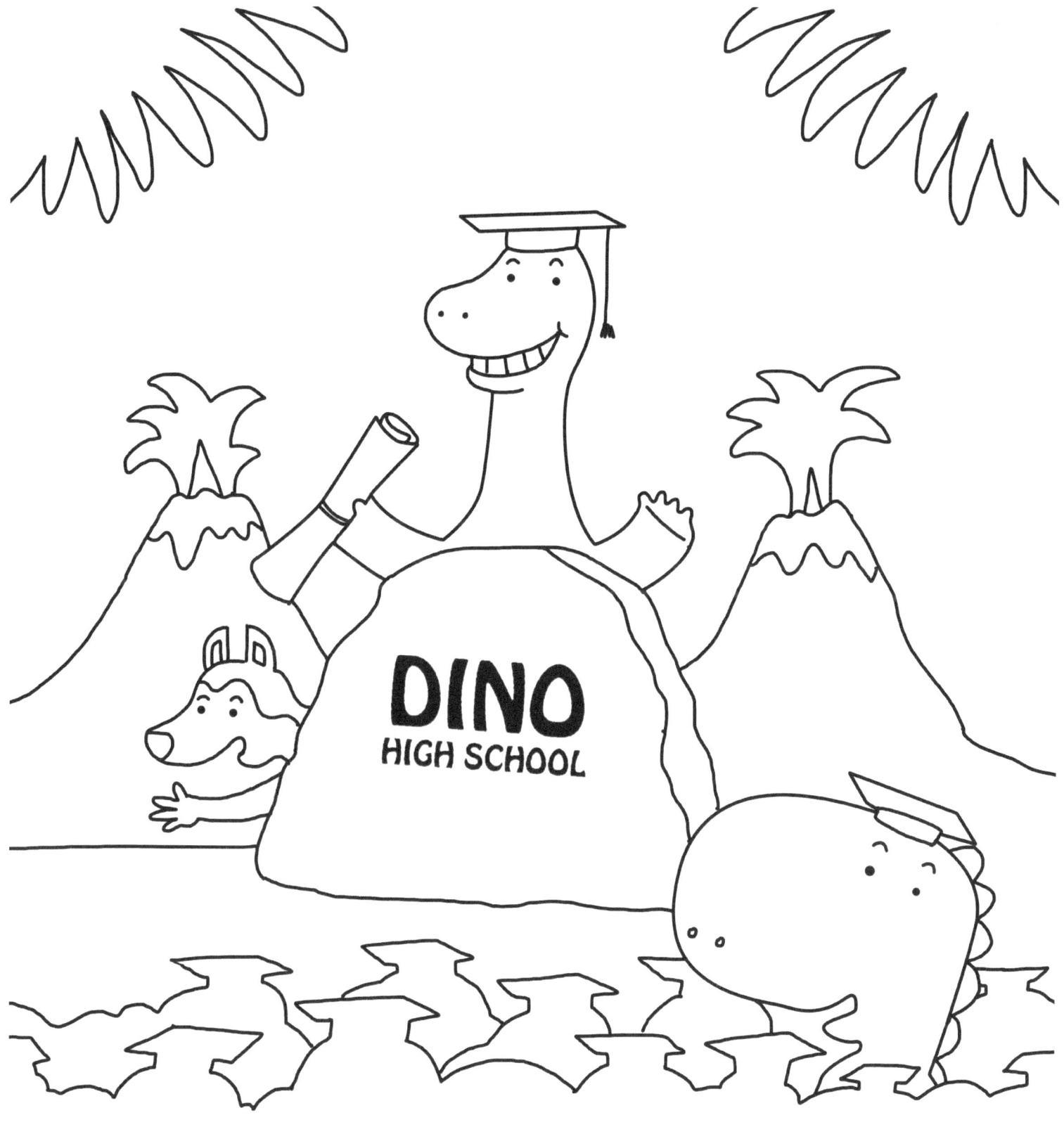

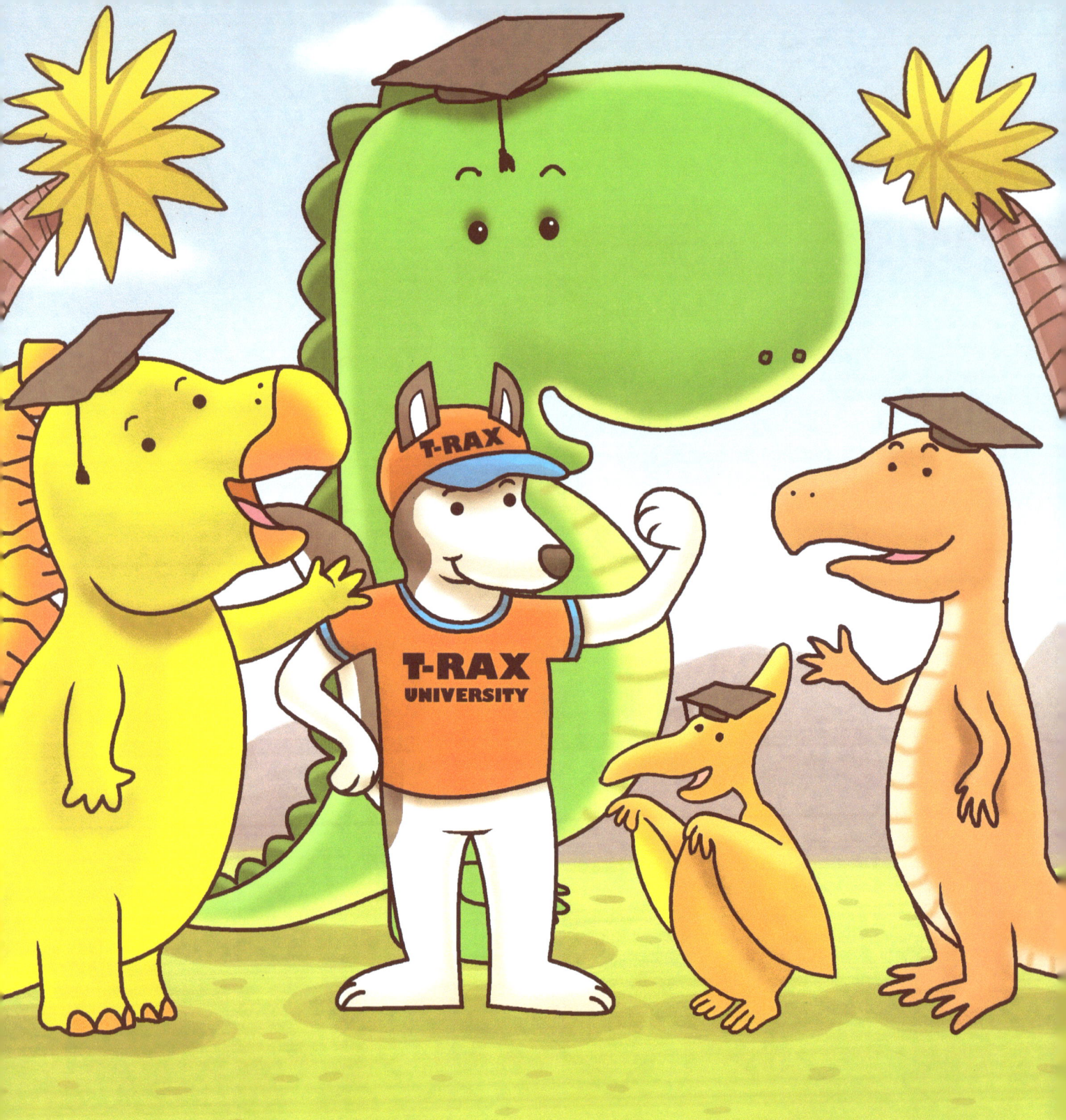

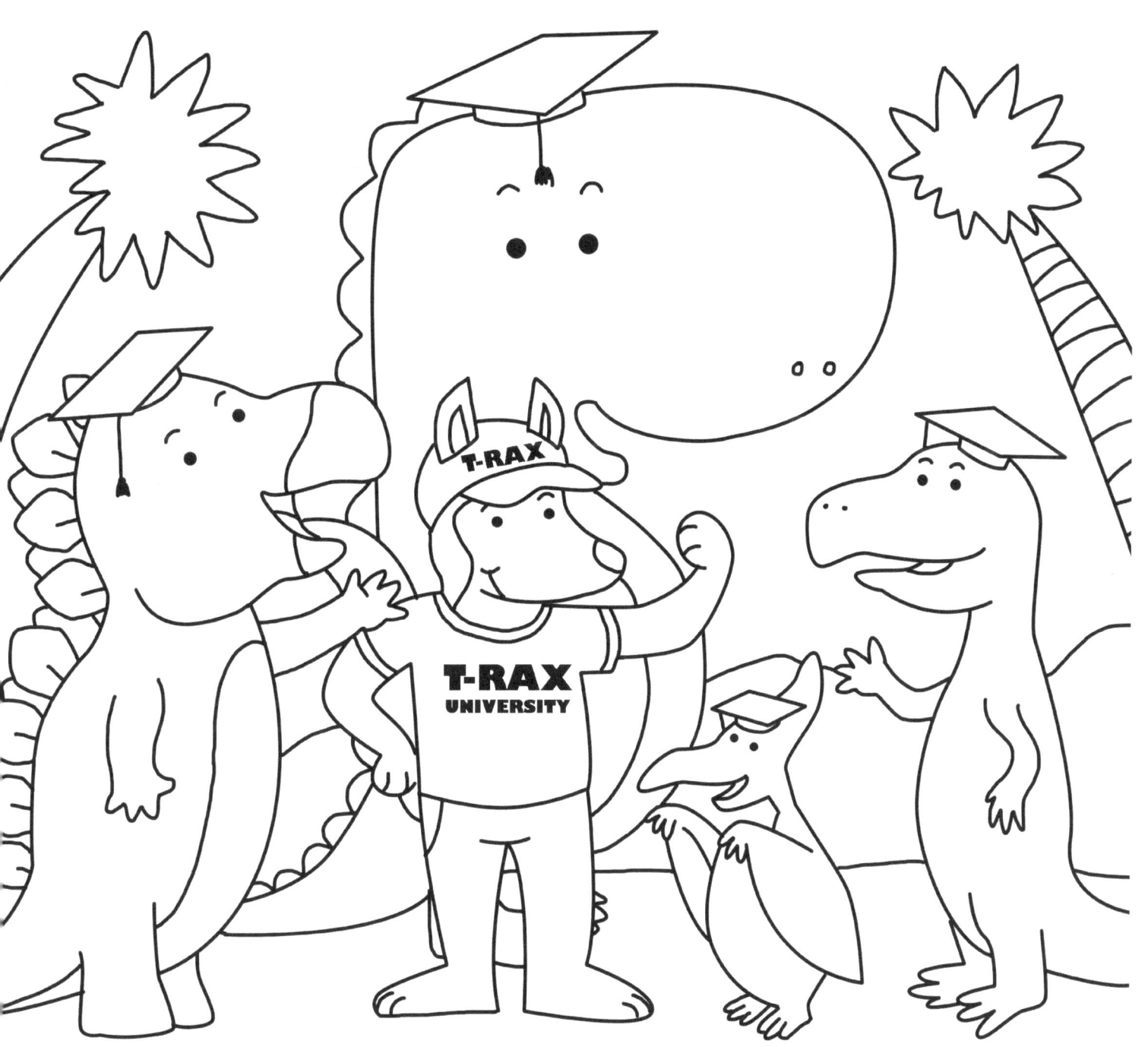

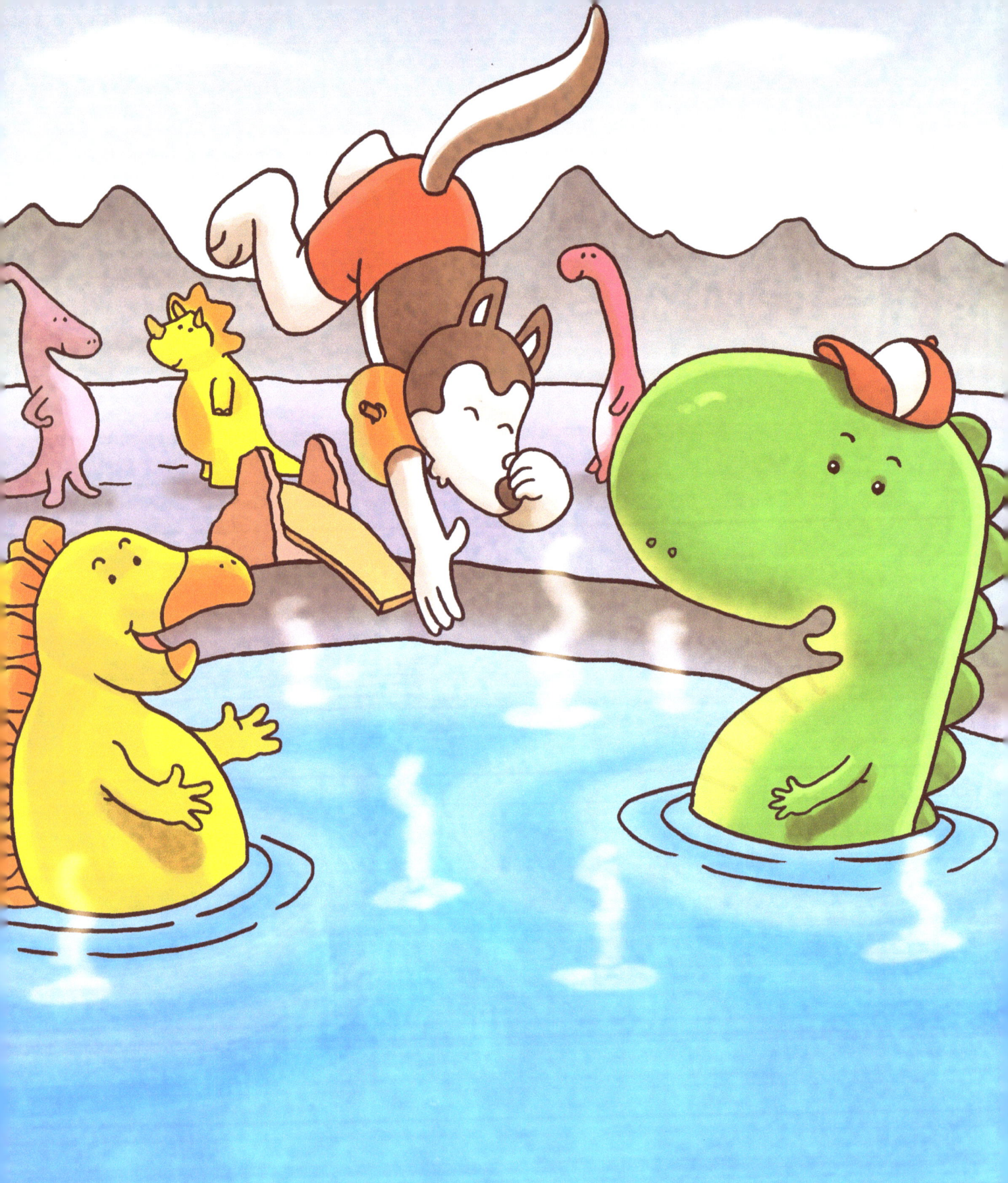

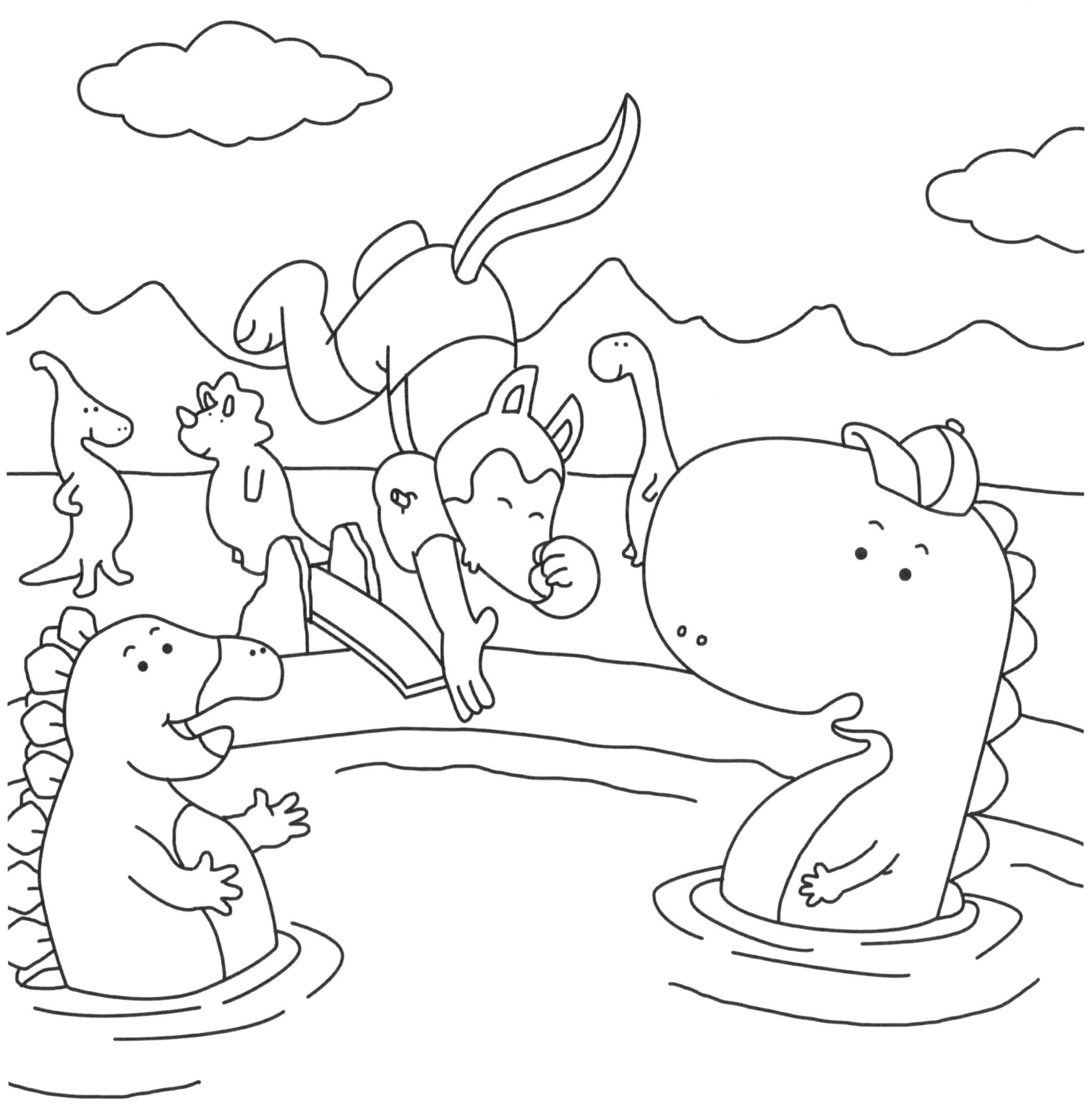

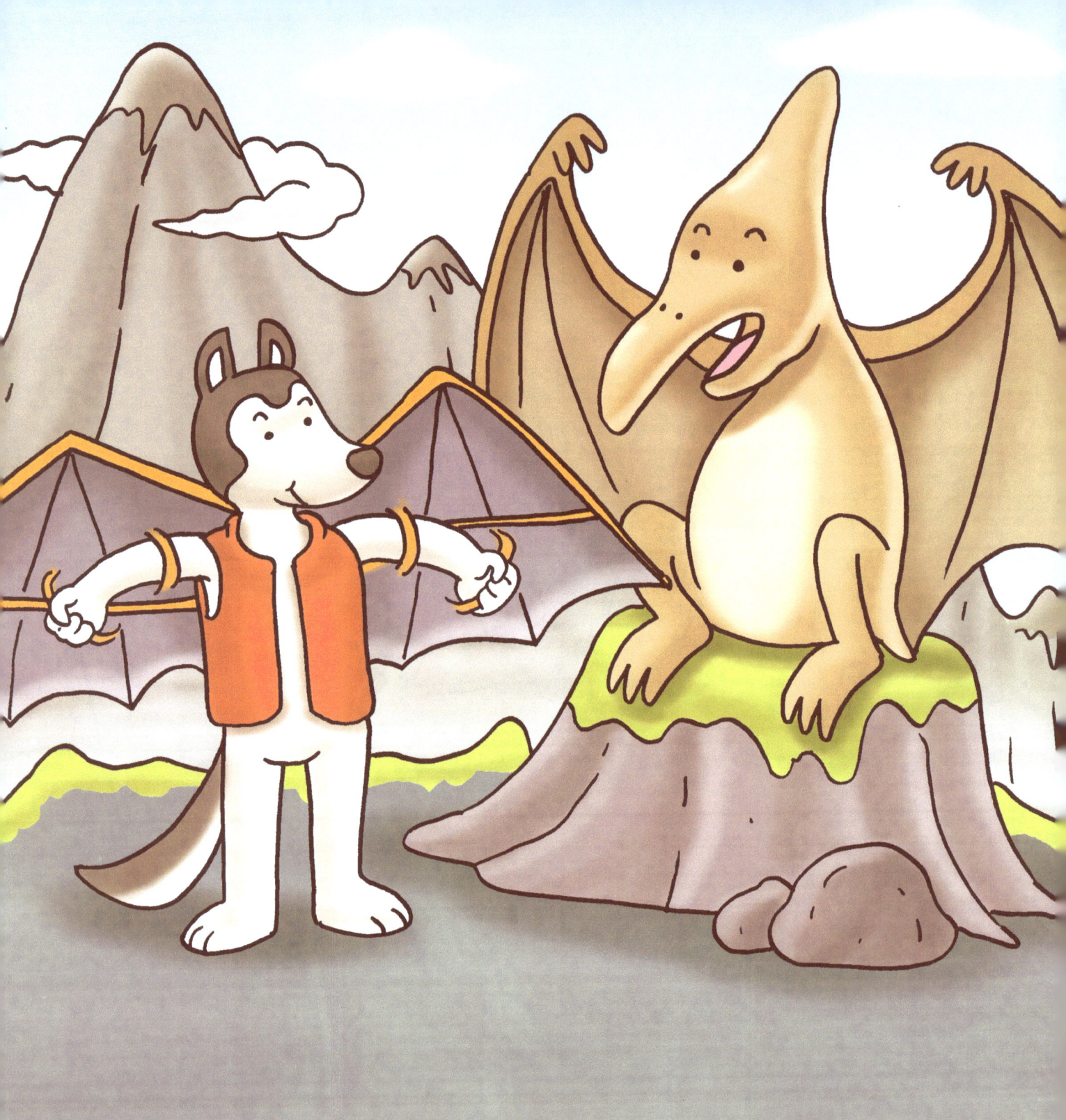

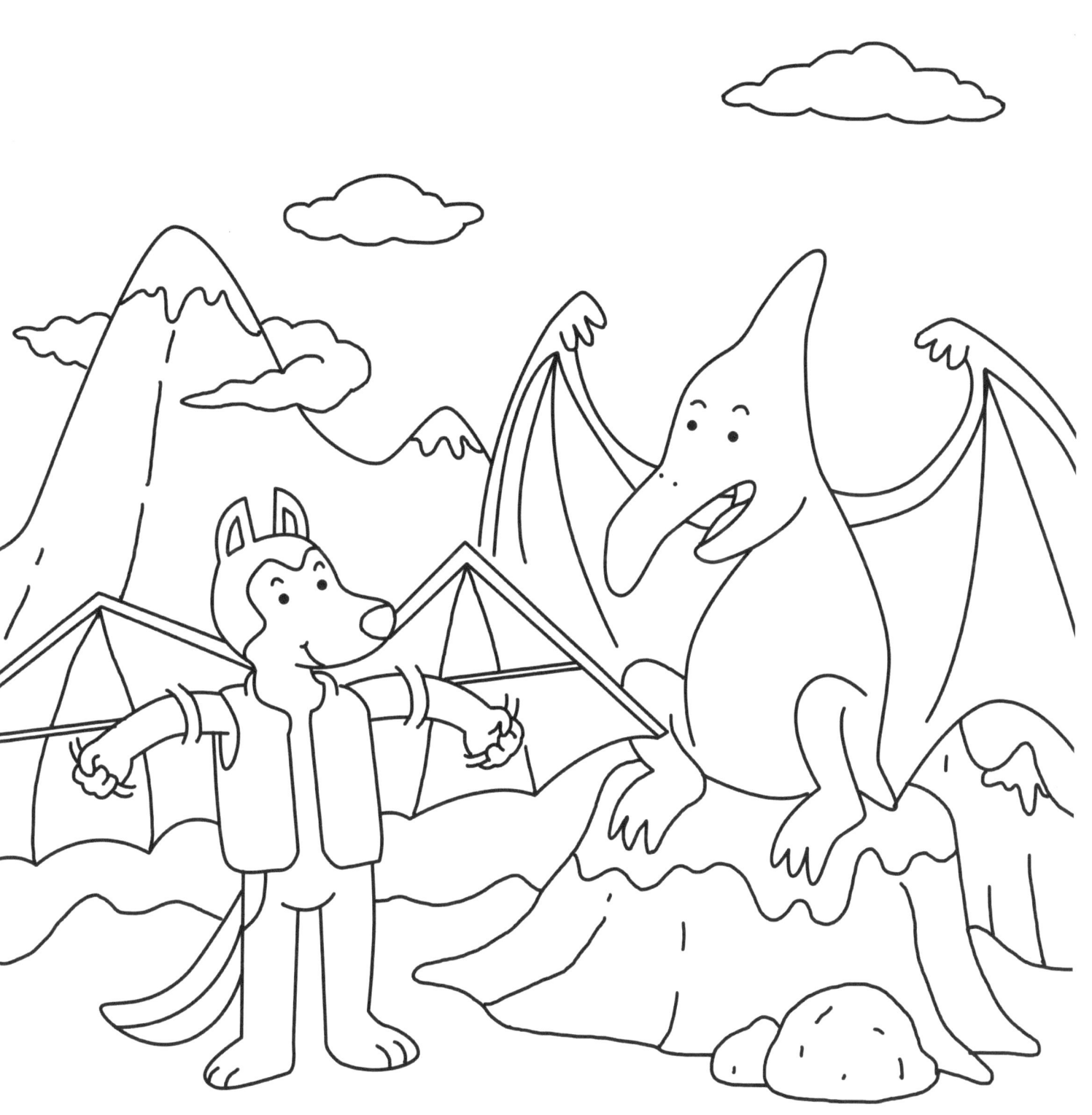

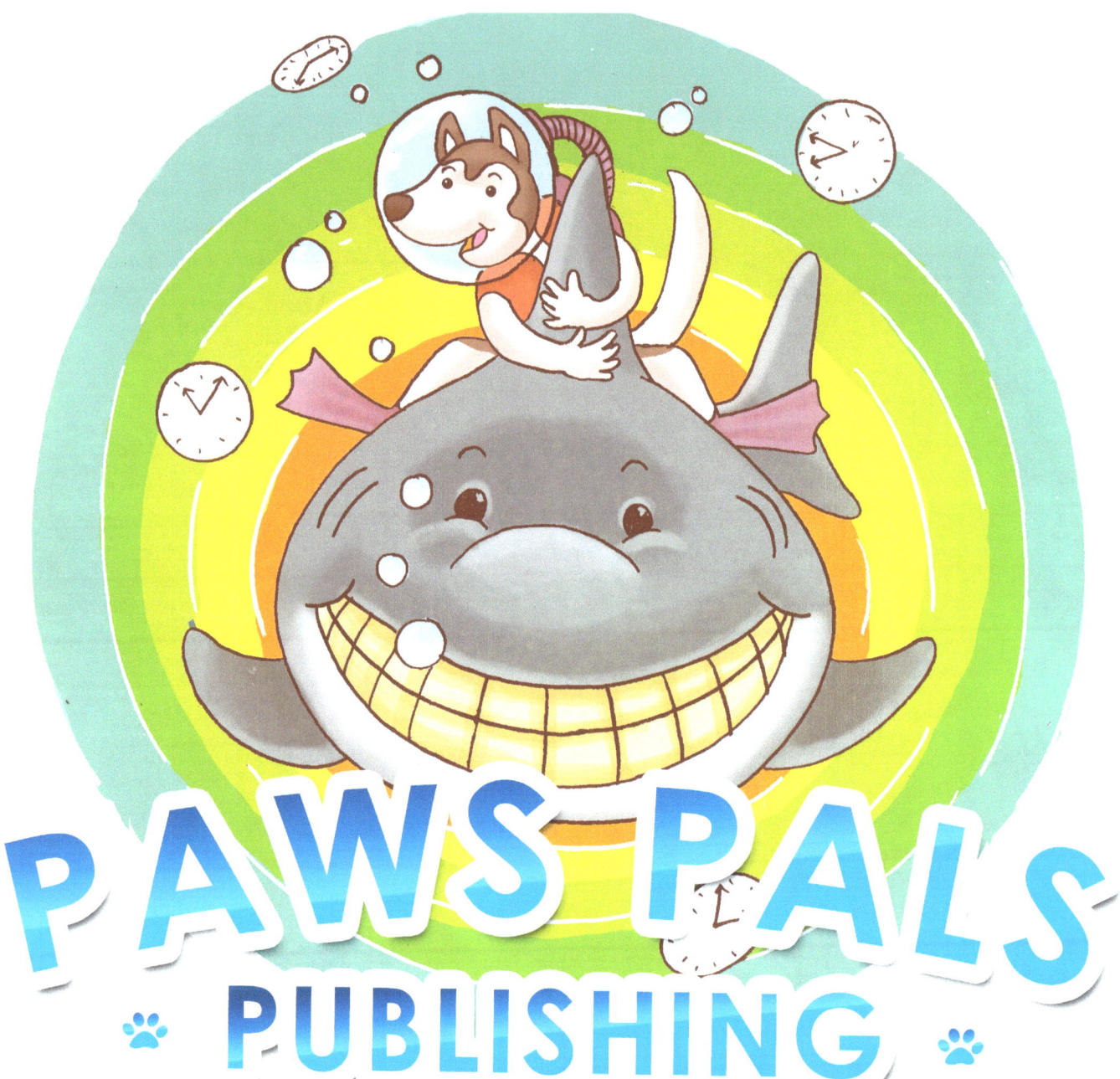

PAWS PALS
PUBLISHING

Published by Andrew Rosenblatt, California December 2015.
www.PawPalsPublishing.com
Library of Congress catalog publication data is available upon request.
ISBN-13: 9781522893059
ISBN-10: 1522893059

Printed in America.

Second Printed Edition: December 22, 2015.

Created by Andrew Rosenblatt

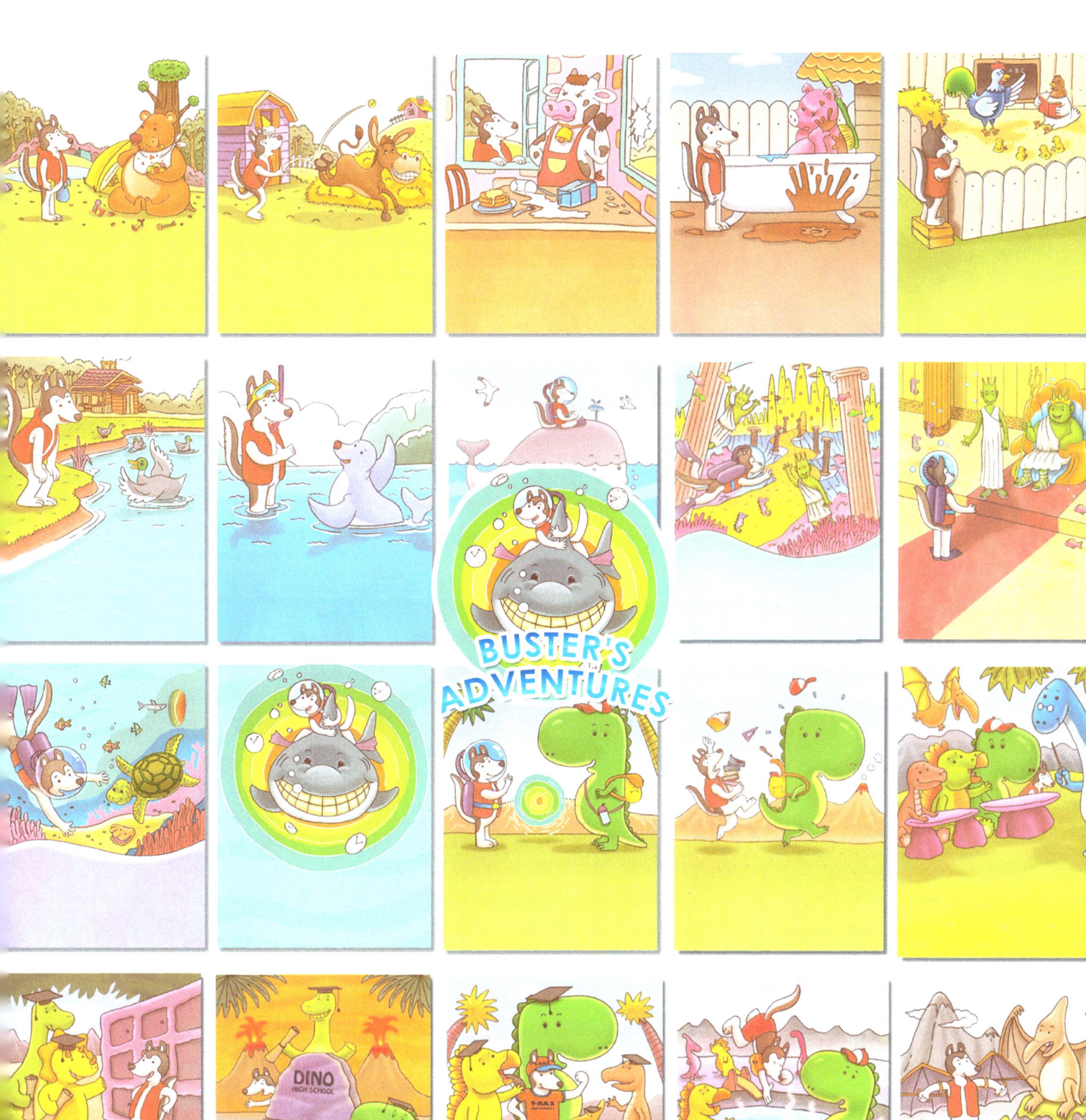